Housewives Guide to becoming Wealthy by:
Creating a Business Plan

By

Cynthia Barber,

And Z. Bey

Hold Harmless Agreement

This book has been published for general educational purposes only. The information contained in this book is not meant to give the exact information needed to run a business as each business is different and requires different components to get started. We have done our best to compile reading material that may be of great use to our readers, but we do not claim to have all the answers to your personal business problems. By reading this book, it is implied that you have read this statement and will hold harmless the authors of the book if any information is deemed obsolete, out of date, or invalid during the time of publishing and in the future publishing. The authors advise its readers to consult with an attorney, or someone in the field of law if additional personalized information is needed for your business needs.

Housewives Guide to becoming Wealthy by: Creating a Business Plan©2018 All Rights Reserved. Z.E.B. This book may not be copied, scanned, accessed in a cloud, a data center, or stored in any electronic, digital, paper or any other format without the express written consent of the author and publisher. For inquiries please contact us at ilifeebooks@gmail.com.

This publication is part of the series Brilliant minds. Whose focus is to teach advanced history, law, business, science, STEM, IB, and college prep courses to the general public. We want you to be ready to advance in life, prior to leaving school.

Housewives Guide to becoming Wealthy by: Creating a Business Plan

Table of Contents

Introduction

Business Plan Package Outline – An exact outline of each section of the business plan

About the Business Plan Questionnaire

1. Writing
2. Research, Research, Research!
3. The Winning Formula
4. Appendix
5. Business Proposal Cover letter

Sample Business Proposal Cover letters

Sample Grant Proposal Cover letters

Business Plan Questionnaire

- Executive Summary-
   a. How does your business address a need?
   b. What want or need does your product / service address, and How? Why do you have the best solution for addressing that need?
- Company Description –
   a. How big is the market and how big will you grow?
- Organization and Management
   a. Who's on your team?
- Marketing and Sales Mgmt.
   a. Essential Marketing Strategies
- Products/ Services
   a. What's so different about what you have to offer?
- Banking Relationships and Current Investors.
- Financials

-
    a. Other ways to look for Financing
- Summary of Company Growth and Market highlights
    a. How will you measure success?
- Summary of Management and Future plans
    a. Visual Map
    b. Goals
- Appendix
    a. Budget sheet Considerations
    b. Additional templates and assistance
    c. Final Thoughts

Ten Ways to Ruin Your Business Plan

Loan Proposal Outline by the SBA

Sample - Business Proposal Letter

Sample - Business Proposal Letter

Sample -Business Proposal Letter

Sample - Business Partnership Letter

Sample - Business Plan for IT Company

Sample – Nonprofit Grant Proposal

Introduction

There are a few things that happen when a person begins thinking about starting a business.

You've made a habit of settling for low wage jobs that will allow you to pay the bills and maintain your household, yet you do not consider it a career. You may have went to college after high school, but years later realized that the field that you are working in is changing for the worse. Maybe you dreamed of owning your business for quite some time, but didn't know how to get started. Has life finally smacked you in the face with a good dose of reality with the fact that no matter how hard you work for someone else, it will never make you financially secure?

Welcome to the club of Entrepreneurs who are making a difference in their lives every year thanks to the realization that the cost of living is increasing and wages are not keeping up with inflation.

Welcome to the exclusive club of individuals who find it hard to find affordable housing for your family because the cost of rent is well over half your monthly earnings.

Welcome to the growing list of people who cannot afford healthcare and food in the same month, thereby deeming us as the working poor.

The world that we live in is rapidly changing. The American dream has always been to own a home, have a great career and a loving family. Fifty years ago, Community college was the average cost of $60.00 per course.

According to American Advisory Group, The average mortgage in the United States for a brand new home in 1963 costs $19,300. The average income for Americans was $4,396 now its $44,321. Bread was a cost of $0.22 cents, now the average is $2.49. The cost of a brand new car in 1963 was $3,233.00, today average cost for a brand new car is $33,560.

In the 1960's, A person who made the average wages was able to sustain themselves on one paycheck, and look forward to retiring in the ripe golden age of 55.

The cost of living was so low that the average American home was actually able to be paid off within a reasonable amount of years, while homeowners could easily live debt free for the remainder of their lives.

Who knew with the rise of Capitalism and Corporate greed, that in just a few short years, we would have the societal issues we have today.

As of May 28, 2015 - Approximately 52.2 million (or 21.3 percent) of people in the U.S. participated in government assistance programs each month in 2012, according to a U.S. Census Bureau.

These are not people asking for a handout while sitting on their butt's everyday eating Cheetos's. The majority of Welfare recipients are the working poor, who have jobs, yet the job is not paying them enough to cover their basic needs. In fact, in 2012 more than 47.8 percent of families who received food stamp were working (the highest ever), and only 13.2 percent were welfare recipients with no income, according to the US Department of Agriculture.(Oct 14, 2013).

To add to this alarming statistics, the entertainment industry has pushed the idea of living a fabulous single life, as well as exposing sex to our younger generations, in the 1980's-90, so for the first time in a very long time in our history, a large population of children were being raised in single parent households. What a strange coincidence that at the same time the invention of child support, and charging a parent for being absent through the court systems, flourished throughout the country and is doing quite well as a lucrative business for each State to this day.

The majority of the population is living with the symptoms of a society based on capitalistic corporate greed, yet we are not holding those that created these societal issue responsible for some many struggling families. If We the People of these United States, have the right to put people in office who are supposed to have our best interest at heart, by becoming a representative of our areas in which we live, We the People can make a change by participating in Government and the election process.

However, these issues are not going to go away overnight. The best thing a person can do for themselves and their communities is to start a small business. The majority of the U.S. economy is run by small businesses. A small business will enable a person to earn the income they desire by putting in time and effort in a product or service they can provide to the public, as well as employ others at a decent salary, which will give them the skills, and income to make a change in the lives of their families.

According to the New York Stock Exchange, (NYSE) The exchange trades stocks for some **2,800** companies, ranging from blue chips to new high-growth companies. In other words, only the biggest companies who make multi-millions of dollars or more, and are not considered small businesses, are traded on the NYSE. Every other business you see in your communities are small businesses, which can easily be millions for each state.

How is it possible that nearly 2,800 companies have assisted in grossly overcharging the population for goods and services? Corporate greed will always be with us, just like death and taxes.

We must fight a corporation with a corporation. In the United States, we are able to level the playing field in this money driven society by starting a business.

Whether you decide to start full-time business, meaning heads-up and feet grounded, because you have nothing to lose, or you decide to start small by creating a part-time side gig, which you hope will blossom into a full-time, self-sustaining business, it doesn't matter; just start a business.

Our book**, The Housewives Guide to becoming Wealthy by Working from Home** was just the first of many books in a series designed to walk anyone desiring a better life through the process of earning a living by working for themselves.

We are teaching our students how to master Business knowledge in each of our book courses because we see the problems that exist, and we believe we can make a difference by teaching others how to start their own business.

The Business Plans book is designed to enable to reader to answer some specific questions, so that you can easily formulate a working plan of what you would like to do for your business.

If you are a young adult, you may it difficult to decide what you want to go into business doing. The easiest way to solve this issue is to think of what you are good at. Do you have a passion for creating, writing, art, music, etc. What do you believe is you talent that you were born with?

Follow your passion; look at what you can do along those lines that will enable you to earn a living, while loving what you do as a career.

Here are a few questions to get you started:

1. Do you want to sell brand named items that everyone is familiar with?

    If so, you are likely looking to start a wholesale business, whereby you would buy name brand, items such as clothing, household merchandise, jewelry etc. at a discount and resell it to the public for a profit. There are many examples of big named companies who specialize in selling overstock items such as Burlington, TJ Maxx, Marshalls, Ross, and Big Lots. There are companies who buy these items brand new direct from the companies who make them, which typically sell the items in department stores such as Macy's, Dillard's, Sears, etc.

2. Do you want to create new items, improved an existing products/ or do you have an invention?

    If you prefer to start your business career by inventing products or improving on existing products on the market, you will likely need to study the market that you want to provide this item in, and see if it is a strong demand for that product. Generally you can get a Patent as well as Trademark for an invention or idea, but you can easily make residual income selling the idea, or licensing your product to companies that are well established on the field. This can easily bring your product to market much more quickly and efficiently, than someone just starting out without a manufacturing company.

3. Do you want to provide a service such as a Barber, Roofer, Electrician, Plumber or Nail Technician?

These services are also known as trades. Trades typically a business you can do with your hands to make you an income. A mechanic, cosmetologist, electrician, plumber, carpenter are all jobs that can easily turn into a lucrative business for yourself with the correct advertising, marketing, and business support. Although we were told as students that a college educated persons will earn more over a lifetime than someone in a trade that statement is simply not true in today's economy. Instead of you looking for a job to sustain your family, you have the ability to create one with very little training, thereby taking out very little to no student loans debt. As long as you have those hands, you will never be out of a job because that is the way you make money.

The average person use to get hired at a company, work for 20 to 30 years at that same company, then retire. In today's market, the average time a person work at a company is less than five years. What if you were laid off from a job? What happens as you look for another job? Nothing changes. You still have the expenses of a working household however, you will no longer be able to pay for those household expenses, unless you acquire another job. That could take months, or even years to gain employment. If you had a trade, that time being laid off who not affect you financially, because you have the ability to work for yourself by opening up your own business, contract with other businesses, or work for someone else who need your skills in their business.

It's no secret; thanks to the invention of the personal computer, millions of people have become more comfortable by sitting for a living. People no longer wish to work hard, they want an easy job, and the idea of pushing a button for eight hours instead of swinging a hammer, has changed our population permanently. Most of the younger generation do not want to work in the trade field.

Unfortunately, we cannot allow this field in business to go away such as the pony express of Western times. We need electricity to light up the homes in which we live in. We need HVAC technicians, because we want to live comfortable by utilizing heat, and air conditioners. And let's face it, we cannot got back to digging a hole outside, and burying that hole as a means of using the bathroom; we need plumbers.

If you have answered the previous three questions honestly, we can point you in the direction of a path you need to take to achieve your goals. But first, we need to take your dream you see in your mind, and reduce it to words on a piece of paper, also known as a business plan, so others can see your dream, and can assist you in making your dream a reality for you.

The biggest myth when creating a business plan is "The most difficult thing to do when creating a business plan is to research your market." Not really; we can research a market, and provide endless statistics relating to that field of interest within a few seconds thanks to the internet. The most difficult thing is to write why it is a good business to be in for you, in a language that everyone can understand. Some people are great at talking, but not writing. Some of us are natural salesmen. We know all about a product, and its features, and can easily walk you through how to fix a problem if necessary, on an item such as a cellphone, but cannot create a business plan.

This book will assist you tremendously in your quest for relaying to the business world what you intend on doing as a business for the rest of your life.

We sincerely hope that you will take your time, and thoroughly read each question in this book, and provide the answer as it relates to your business, as it will give you the information you need to include in a business plan. We have included some tips along the way to help you in your quest for the perfect business plan, which will be a series of paragraphs below the Headers and questions sections marked with Roman numerals. When writing your business plan, include the sections headers that are in **bold** as well as <u>underlined</u>, with roman numerals, then proceed to answer the questions on that section to build your paragraph about the subject.

After reading this series, we hope that you will share your goals, dreams and successes on our Facebook page:

www.facebook.com/housewivesguidetobecomingwealthy

- The Authors

Percentage of business leadership roles held by women

Arrows indicate change from long-run average

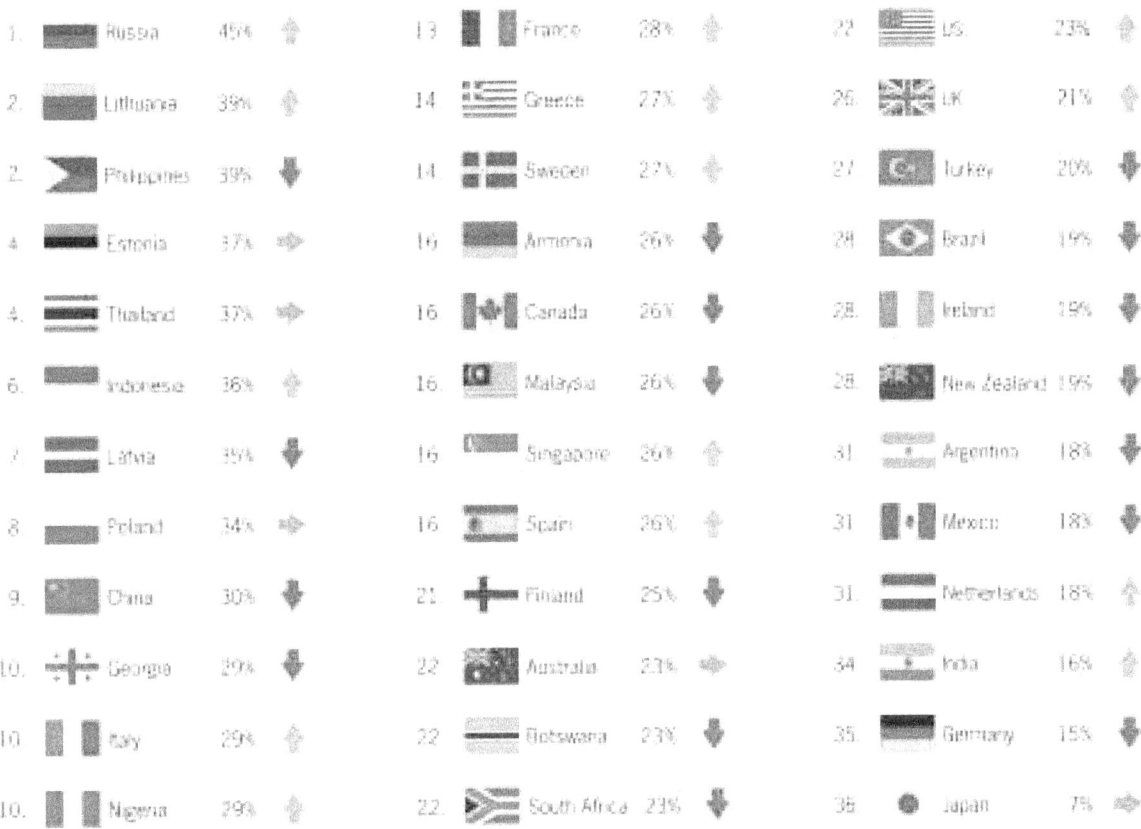

1. As of 2013, 75.1 million women ages 16 and older participated in the U.S. workforce. That comes out to 47.4% of all U.S. civilian labor.

47.4% of all U.S. civilian labor

2. **13.6%** women in management

15.5% of men

Of those women, 13.6% of them were employed in management, business, and financial-related positions in 2013, compared with 15.5% of men.

3. Businesses owned by women provide **23 MILLION JOBS**

As far back as 2009, businesses owned by women were responsible for providing 23 million jobs (that was 16 percent of all the jobs in the U.S. that year) as well as contributing $2.86 trillion to the U.S. economy based on total annual revenue data.

2.86 TRILLION contributed to the U.S. economy

Business Plan Package Outline

Business Proposal letter - Personalized Cover letter addressed to the Investor/ Bank

Cover Sheet: Business Name, Address, Phone Number, Principals

Table of Contents – Sections of your business plan and the pages the section starts on.

- **Executive Summary-**
- **Company Description** –
- **Organization and Management**
- **Marketing and Sales Mgmt.**
- **Products/ Services**
- **Banking Relationships and Current Investors.**
- **Financials**
- **Summary of Company Growth and Market highlights**

*Please attach to the end of this section [Projected Financial Statements, Income Statements, Cash Flow Statements Balance Sheets of existing accounts, Assumptions to Projected Financial Statements, Break Even Analysis, and Sources and Uses of Funds]

- **Summary of Management and Future plans**
- **Appendix**

**Attach the following information at the end of your completed business plan document.

1. Include your resume for yourself and all of your officers.
2. It will include letters and /or statements from your existing credit accounts in good standing and personal financial information if possible.
3. A copy of your incorporation documents
4. A copy of licenses, permits, and DBA documents, if applicable.

5. Credit report if requested. (Some banks or funding sources will ask for a copy of your credit report. It will be listed in this section of the business plan.)
6. Contact information and/or company profile of accountants or an accounting firm you wish to hire.
7. Consultants with consultant profile and contact information you plan on using for your business
8. Will you be hiring a payroll service such as ADP? Who did you contact at ADP, and what is their contact information?
9. If you are a non-profit, include letters of support from existing established nonprofits will be attached to the business plan in this section.
10. Historical financial statements if it's an existing business
11. Previous tax returns for at least three years
12. Reference letters from business associates and partners
13. Personal financial statements, and or tax returns
14. Facilities Diagram, if you do not currently have a physical place of business currently.
15. Existing contracts
16. Purchase orders, if applicable
17. Letters of Intent, if applicable
18. Budget Sheets
19. Business loan application

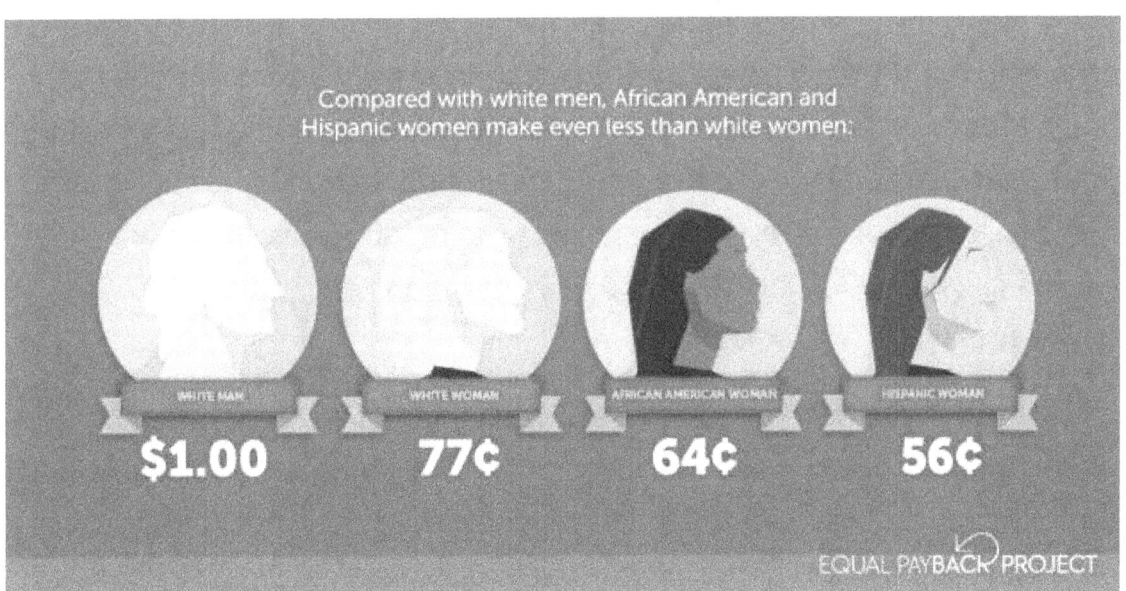

About the Business Plan Questionnaire

Writing

Everyone we give this Business Plan to will gladly judge you. Their impression, good or bad, will be solely based upon the information you provide in this business plan. It will not only show to a potential investor if it is a good business to invest in, it will also show the investor if it is a good idea to trust you as a person to go into business with. Unless you are seeking financial assistance from friends, and family to get you started, these investors will likely know nothing about you, and how you do business.

How do they know that a person will not take the money they are given and run off to another city? How can they trust a person to use the money for the business, and not use it for personal shopping sprees? How do they know that you have the experience or education in this business to make it successful? Investors can get a sense of who you are, while learning if you are a good person to be in business with by utilizing our business plans.

Each of the questions below are unique, and has been systematically placed in the order they are supposed to be in. All business plans have the same outline. As you read the following questions, you'll notice that some of the information on this form will be required, as it applies to all business plans, while other questions may not fit your business model. Skipping a vital question, and not doing the research to see if it applies to your business, will likely cost you a new business relationship. We do not want to give an impression to a potential investor that we are not knowledgeable about the business. In this instance, the more information you can give the better picture they will be able to see about your experience in the market, your personality and professionalism.

Research, Research, Research!

A quick tip is to do research and include the average when it comes to costs as well as a conservative growth projection. We can never predict events that may happen in the future which can cause our business expenses to increase, decrease or may cause us to go out of business.

Wildfires and mudslides have been taking our entire neighborhoods and cities in recent years. The protest of Monsanto genetically engineered food product has alarmed millions of people who refuse to support buying the cheapest fruits and vegetables not labeled organic. New federal legislative laws enacted in early 2018 promising to crack down on dispensaries. All of these events happened within the last 12 months leaving businesses as well as families in jeopardy of losing everything they built. There will be times when it seems your business is doing great, then politics, the environment, public opinions, or the markets will change, so we must be able to put money aside in these hard times when events happen.

The Winning Formula

Mistakes can, and will be made in the early stages of starting a business. With proper planning, in the first stages of establishing a business, we can avoid becoming a struggling business. In business there is an old saying that says, "Do not go into any business you cannot make at least three times what you put out in costs, back from the customer." I definitely use this equation when I am deciding if it will be profitable to start a business. Here's why:

- One third of the expenses will go towards purchasing the goods / creating the product.
- Two thirds of the business finances will go into paying staff and operational costs.
- The last third will go into your savings, so that you can re-purchase the product.
- All other profits outside of this formula can be saved for future events and to grow your business.

It is a common mistake to start a business, and not get into the habit of paying yourself a salary. The finances may not initially be there, but add the expense to your business plan so that when you can make a little money from your business, you know what to do with it. If you use the formula above, the expenses of the staff and operational costs are already accounted for in each sale, so you do not have to struggle to keep the business in business.

Other financial experts say that "It's alright to just make the money you put out, because you have the ability to increase your sales as time goes by." We cannot sustain a business, and our households, without taking care of ourselves in the process. Unless you have a tremendous amount of unlimited money to invest in the process, the financial supply will eventually run dry. If it has been a long time since the business has turned a profit, you'll likely need to call in an expert to assist you in figuring out what we can do to increase the sales, and decrease the operational costs.

Appendix

At the end of a business plan is the last section called the Appendix. It is typical for a Business Plan to include the resumes of the persons incorporating the business, business partners, founders, executives, etc. in this section. Have this information ready from each of your officers as it will be a piece of vital information that we need to include in our business plans. Simply print copies of these documents and add it to the **end** of your business plan along with a **Budget Sheet** for your business to complete the package. There will be some examples of resumes outlines as well as sample budget projections at the end of this book to assist you in the final stages of creating a business plan.

Business Proposal Cover letter

Every good Business plan will include a cover letter, on the company's letterhead stationery, to the potential investor prior to starting the business plan meeting. Of course this requires you to do a little research in finding the name and address of the person you will be sitting down to discuss your business plan with prior to the meeting. However, we do want to show that we are professional, and we took the time out to write a personalized letter about your business.

Some investors during these meetings immediately look at numbers, projections, and educational backgrounds. This is your one and possibly only chance, you will have to make a great first impression by:

- Thanking them for this opportunity to review your business plan.
- Explain the reason why you have decided to open a business. (Using one or two paragraphs).

- Explain why you believe the investor or (bank) and your business would be good partnership. (Using one or two paragraphs).
- Give the amount of money you are seeking and what you will use it for. Show your enthusiasm about the business by explaining the need for the product or service. (Using one or two paragraphs).
- Close by thanking them for their time
- Sign your name

The next few pages are sample Business letter Proposal letters for you to review.

SAMPLE BUSINESS PROPOSAL COVER LETTER

DATE

Name of Investor or lending officer at a Lending Institution
Name of Bank or Lending Institution
Address of Bank etc.
City, State, Zip Code

Dear Mr/Ms. Name of lender or investor,

I am submitting my business plan to you in the hope of receiving a start-up loan for $50,000. I learned about your history of funding recycling centers, and my proposal takes the business to the next level. We will be a source for other businesses who want to use recycled products or use waste material to recycle into their own products. According to our research, consumers are looking for businesses that use environmentally friendly products.

I have $10,000 that I plan to invest in this business. As stated in the plan, we aim to make $5,000 profit the first year and reinvest in the business to widen our clientele. We will be the first company in the city to offer this service, so we hope to be well established before competing companies enter the industry.

My brother, Name of Brother, and I are working together to make this business a success. We have worked for the last five years in Name of Company, where they manufacture plastic sheeting for construction companies from recycled plastic.

As stated in the plan, I will collect the waste material and my brother will manage the accounts. We plan to employ office help and waste collection help. We have contacted several recycling centers in the city who agree to sell us their recyclable waste. We have found a warehouse available to rent when we go forward with the business.

Thank you for your time and consideration in this matter. I hope you will review my business plan. If you have any questions or would like to discuss the plan, I can be reached at 555-123-4567 or at Name@email.com. I would be happy to meet you at any time that is convenient for you.

Sincerely,

Signature of Applicant
Name of Applicant Printed
Business Plan Enclosed

SAMPLE BUSINESS PROPOSAL COVER LETTER

Sender's Name
Sender's Address
City, State, Zip Code

DATE

Receiver's Name
Receiver's Title
Receiver's Address City, State, Zip Code

Dear Name of Receiver,

I am the Sales Director of Name of Company, and I met you at the Name of Conference or Event last month. A representative of our sales team, Name of Person, will be in Los Angeles between DATE and DATE and would like to meet you on any of those days for 30 minutes if possible between 9am – 12pm.

He has done research on your company and believes he has a mutually beneficial business proposition he would like to discuss with you.

Would it be convenient for you, or someone you delegate, to meet NAME on one of these days? I will call you in a few days to discuss any details or questions you may have and arrange an alternative time if required.

Sincerely,

Sender's signature

Sender's Name printed
Sender's Title

Sample Grant Proposal Cover letter

[Date]

[Name]

[Title]

[Foundation Name]

[Address]

[City, State, Zip]

[Dear Mr./Ms. _____,]

We are requesting $ (Dollar Figure) for a community-built play space in our neighborhood, to be located at (Exact Address and Location). We believe this request fits under your giving area of (Foundation's Specific Giving Area) because (Detail Reasons).

Our vision and mission are central to our efforts in generating funds for this play space: (Detail Organization's Mission and Vision).

A new, safe and accessible play space is needed in our community for the following reasons:

(Detail Why a Play space is needed).

With this grant, we will build a play space with (Number of Play Activities) play activities. This play space will serve (Number of Families Served) families in the neighborhood and (Number of Youth) youth. This community-built play space will employ (Number of Volunteers Needed) volunteers who will actually build the structure under the guidance of a certified installer and play equipment representative. We have collaborated with (Number of Businesses Collaborated With) local businesses and organizations to help us make this dream come true.

I will call to confirm the receipt of this letter and to answer any questions. I can be reached at

(Phone Number) should you need to get in touch with me.

Sincerely,

[Contact person] [Director/President of Organization]

[Title] [Title]

Sample Grant Proposal Cover letter

Date

Name, Title (Grantmaker Contact)
Foundation, Bank, Corporation (Grantmaker)
Address
City, State, Zip Code

RE: Name of Grant

(Name of Organization) is pleased to submit this request for your review. We look forward to your partnership in our cooperative efforts to rebuild (Name of Community).

Our proposal requests $ (amount of request) to launch our creative homeowner down payment revolving loan program to provide a 50/50 match down payment to enable the low- and moderate-income residents of (Name of Community) the opportunity to own their own homes.

Our homeownership down payment loan model is creative in promoting homeownership opportunities for the tenants of (Name of Organization) rental housing. This (Name of Grant) program supports the (Name of Grantmaker) objectives to promote community resident home-ownership opportunities.

We have secured $ (Amount) funds to seed the program, have pre-qualified more than 100 community residents for down payment loans, and bring a 50/50 match for every dollar in this request.

For the last fifteen years, (Name of Organization) has successfully produced affordable housing in (Name of Organization). We have delivered more than 1000 units of affordable housing to our community. Your ongoing investment in our housing programs and projects will enable us to continue to effectively serve our impoverished community, and its working poor residents.

Thank you for your interest in (Name of Organization). We envision building upon our collaborative success by developing our homeownership down payment loan program with you.

Sincerely,

(Name of CEO/Board Chair)
(Title of CEO/Board Chair)

Business Plan Questionnaire

{ XYZ company name,}

Physical address or PO Box, phone number

email address, and website address}

I. <u>**Executive Summary-**</u>

1. What is the name of your business? Do you have another name you will be doing business as, if so list the name.
2. Mission Statement – What is your mission statement?
3. What are your Objectives?
4. What is your Goal for the business?

How does your business idea address a need?

This is where you get to explore the true potential of your new idea. There are two basic types of demand in the marketplace—a "want" and a "need." A business that addresses a need is always more promising than one that addresses a want. In the case of a market need, there's pre-existing "pent-up" demand, and creating awareness is all that's required to catalyze the sales of your offering. A market need creates "pull" in the marketplace, and the customer literally pulls your product, or service through the system to satisfy his or her need.

In the case of a market want, you'll be required to "push" your product onto consumers, and this usually requires expensive advertising, and marketing campaigns in order to encourage and influence the sale. There are varying degrees of "want" in the marketplace so try to get a sense of the degree to which the market wants your product or service. A hair product, the latest cellular phone, or the most fashionable shoes every child is wearing are all examples of a wants, but can be a very lucrative business to go into as everyone strives to look their best at all times. Obviously the more the "want" approaches "need," the better. Basics such as food, shelter, and clothing are examples of market needs, while goods like jewelry, video games, and gourmet high end food products such as smoked salmon, caviar, and Cuban cigars are examples of market wants.

What want or need does your product / service address, and How? Why do you have the best solution for addressing that need?

The hardest thing we can do is to take a look at our ideas with a sensible mind, and figure out if your idea is revolutionary, evolutionary, or simply a copycat.

A revolutionary idea, something that really is different, often means you have a far greater chance for becoming an overnight success which means, more potential revenue and profits. But revolutions typically come with a lot of risk. Don't underestimate how challenging it is to educate consumers and change their behavior before they see the need for your product. It's often said among seasoned entrepreneurs that you can easily spot pioneers in the business world; they're the ones with all the arrows in their backs. They may have a winning idea and can produce a product to go to market. Other businessmen who have been in business just as long, with more manufacturing capabilities, and lower costs, can take your design, copy the product, and change a few ingredients and /or design, so that it will not infringe upon your trademark rights. Be clear in your business plan about how much pioneering you'll have to do before people understand how and why your product is a winner.

An evolutionary idea typically has less upside than a revolutionary one, but your odds are better of getting the business up and running and into a stable mode relatively fast. With an evolutionary idea, the bigger burden is making clear to your customers what distinguishes you from the rest of the competition.

Examples of this could be a new baby toy or baby food. There are thousands of companies making baby products / food on the market. Why is your product different? Is your food organic? Is it flashed steamed? Is your containers BPA free? So are a few hundred other baby products. So what can you bring to the market that can allow a shopper/ consumer to buy your product?

II. **Company Description** –

1. Date the business began?
2. What led you to start this business? Is it a For-profit or a non-profit business?
3. Who is the target market (or businesses you plan to do business with)?
4. Who has the problem in the target Market and what is your solution?
5. What makes your business different from the others in the business? List similarities and differences.
6. What will the industry do without your service?
7. What is your expertise and qualifications?

How big is the market and how big will you grow?

Exploring the market and understanding the growth potential for your product / service is essential. To get a handle on this, we have to understand the demographics of people in your target market. Are you seeking to do business on a local level, just you home country, or worldwide? We can distribute customers into several categories:

Low - Low level of need,   Medium - medium level of need

High - high level of needs.

We can construct a target, like the archery target you may have tried to hit as a kid, except the "bull's-eye" in this case is your winners circle—the *target* market that we will focus our initial marketing and sales efforts.

Once you've penetrated that inner circle, you can grow bigger by broadening your offerings, (adding new products or services to your business), your marketing, and sales efforts to include the people with a medium level of need etc.

To get a fix on the degree of need that may exist for what you're going to offer, try to figure out which market is easiest to penetrate. Is the market growing? If so, by how much? Can you figure out if the market is already saturated, meaning millions of businesses produce this product, mature, as it is nothing new but has a proven track record in sales, or shrinking, as most fads such as silly bands and fidget spinners are here today, and gone tomorrow.

We find that a great deal of the information you'll need can be readily gathered over the Internet. The information you'll find online is free in most cases, but there are also studies online that have been performed by major consulting firms. These studies are often available for purchase and can be really helpful in facilitating a deeper understanding of a market and your company's opportunity within it. When a company really understands its markets, it can produce a plan of attack on the market, and systematically take out your competition.

Researching your growth potential will give you a sense of how big your company can be as well as help you set targets for rolling out new products and or services.

A great example that I have noticed recently in the last year is a small franchise called Charming Charlie's. Initially this store had a great idea to just sell primarily jewelry to its customers. As you look throughout the stores, it seemed that purses, shoes, and clothing was a secondary thought, but a good one as it's stores are designed like a closet. What do you have more of in your closet, jewelry or clothing? Hopefully clothing, however in these stores, clothing is scarce, and can only be purchased in average sizes. Hoping to diversify their offering of products in te store over the last year, they have launched a make-up line and now sell everything from blush, to lipstick in their stores. What a great idea, however, I am sure the owners of this business spent millions of dollars to create these products and bring them to market with their own brand stamped on the product. However, the most sensible solution to this problem of low sales would have been to utilize what relationship they already have with their manufacturers, and create, more up to date shoes, clothing and accessories for the stores, and offer bigger sizes, as the average American woman is a size 14-16; not a size small, medium or large. Although the taste of the clothing is on target with today's market, the offerings are not, therefore customers are not buying the clothing as much as the jewelry. Diversification is key in business.

A note of caution: Don't get caught using "Chinese math." It's all too easy to pile up grandiose numbers for your market size. The phrase "Chinese math" was used back in the 1990s during an era when consumer product companies were eyeing the billions of consumers in China. But eyeing was about all they could really do. Even though there were billions of potential consumers there, they remained just that—*potential,* not real customers of your business. This was largely because there was no viable way to get access to them.

Let's say you wanted to market water purifiers to remote rural populations in a developing country such as Guatemala. There is a great need in those areas for clean drinking water. Imagine the conditions of living on unpaved roads in villages, crowded in huts or barely livable structures without TVs, magazines, or billboards. Since they primarily commute to work on bicycles, radio advertising was also out of the question. Not to mention that most media in developing countries was is controlled by their governments. Freedom of information and disposable income are hard to come by. Even though the market was vast, the obstacles for selling water purifiers to those *potential* customers would have been insurmountable.

Avoid using "Chinese math" in your market estimates. Get real about how many people there are in your market, and about whether you can reach them effectively.

III. <u>Organization and Management</u>

1. Name the Founders, their job titles, and functions they will perform.
2. List licenses, and accreditations, for the industry and city that you have obtained to open your business. (Do not make this a very long paragraph for each of the officers. Highlight key information and we will refer to the resumes for further information.)
3. List the Number of Employees (initially and list the maximum amount needed)
4. Proposed location of the business as well as any prospective branches, DBA's or Subsidiaries
5. What is the Description of the facility or the facility you need? Why are these areas best suited for you and your business?
6. How will you manage your business? What are the offices/positions that will be available?
7. What are the expected qualifications of each open position?
8. What is your hiring process? Do they have to pass a background Check? Will you perform drug tests?

Who's on your team?

This is where thinking about who can assist you in taking your dreams into reality. One of the key factors that'll separate your business from the competition will be the people you choose to work with. Give serious review to the team you pick to start and run your business. Your success depends in large part on them. You may not have an advanced degree in manufacturing a product, or over 20 years of experience in a service industry, but if you can find a person who does have the experience and agree to assist you in brining your product or service to market, his years of information and educational experiences will become a priceless asset to you.

Your business plan is the place to sort out your areas of expertise. Maybe you do have a great idea in a market you don't know much about. If this is the case, hire someone who has expertise in that market as a consultant. Include their services in your business plan and the budget sheet if you are planning to hire someone in the future. Ex: Bill spent four years learning to be a paralegal. He spent time getting the expertise and credentials he needed to create a contract paralegal service. In a formal business plan, investors will want to know that you and your team have a deep knowledge of the business you are entering into.

If you won't be hiring a lot of people in the beginning stages, we still suggest you write up a wish list of folks that you'd like to hire. It really helps to have a dream team waiting in the wings. Finally, if you're doing it alone, don't forget to write down how you plan to outsource work that you simply can't do yourself. Examples could be utilizing contract websites such as Freelancer, Upwork, Fiverr, all of which are wildly popular websites whereby companies hire individuals to perform daily, as well as one time tasks.

Thanks to technology, there are more business models to choose from than ever before. Today you can start a business part-time or full-time, at home, online or in a brick-and-mortar commercial location.

The key is to choose a business model that fits your current lifestyle. This will ensure that you spend the right number of hours each week, take the right level of risk (some models involve more risk than others), are practical in terms of your financial investment, which will allow you to gain the experience as well as the kind of satisfaction and success you're after.

How much time do you want to devote to your business?

When you go for a full-time business model, you leave behind whatever you were doing previously to commit yourself completely to your start-up. When you make this leap, expect to spend more hours working than you ever did working for someone else.

Alternatively, you can start up a business part-time. With this model, you adapt your business to time-consuming obligations you already have, such as your day job, parenting responsibilities, or any other activities that would keep you from making your startup your primary focus.

Once you've determined whether you see yourself as a part-time or full-time entrepreneur, consider our list of business model options.

1. Home-based

   Drawing upon technology, you can create a legitimate and competitive business from home. It's part of our culture now, accounting for more than half of all businesses. Home-based businesses can be run full-time or part-time, and may or may not be web-based.

2. Brick-and-mortar

This is a business with a classic physical location outside of the home. It involves a dedicated facility - whether retail, wholesale, service or manufacturing.

3. E-Commerce

   In this model, you don't have foot traffic in your business, only traffic to your website. You sell your product through your website to consumers or to other businesses.

4. eBay (Or Amazon.com or other auction sites)

   A sub-category of e-commerce, but one big enough to consider on its own, eBay can serve as a location for your online store, and allow you to tap into its huge marketplace.

5. Franchising

When you choose a franchise business model, you use someone else's proven business concept as your entrepreneurial roadmap. Typically you pay an upfront fee, as well as a portion of revenues over time, to the franchisor.

Upside

- **Lower risk** than opening an independent brick-and-mortar business, because franchising provides you with a streamlined process to start your business, as well as support for marketing, business plan samples and estimates, assistance with real estate issues, and staff training.
- Provides you with a **recognized, established brand** to attract customers more quickly.
- To illustrate the lower risk inherent in a franchise, **success rates** for franchises are higher than non-franchise businesses.

Downside

- You've got to be able to pay the upfront franchise fees.
- Franchise guidelines can be strict and limit your ability to get creative with your business.
- Your financial upside is somewhat limited because you must pay your franchisor a cut of your profits

6. Licensing your product

If you're working a day job and don't want to start a business, you can still take advantage of your great product idea by licensing the product to another company that has the entire infrastructure in place to properly manufacture, market and sell the product.

Upside

- **Lower risk** because you can work on your product part-time.
- **Lower cost** because your main expense is production of a prototype and testing the product to make it attractive to potential licensees (rather than the cost involved in setting up an entire business to make, market and sell the product).
- **Freedom** to move on to the next big business idea - if you do successfully license your product idea, you could receive royalties long after you've stopped working on the product!

Downside

- Finding the right licensee takes tenacity and determination, and can take a long time – don't quit your day job!
- Unless your product gets sold in a significant enough volume by the company to which you license it, the amount of royalties you receive can be low or non-existent.
- It's extremely difficult to get through the door of big companies to start a negotiation. That's partly why less than 3% of all patented ideas actually make it to market through licensing agreements.
- Multi-level marketing

Multi-level marketing (MLM) is a marketing and distribution structure. People at the top sell to those below them, who in turn sell to those below them. The higher up you are in this structure, the more money you can make. The challenge with MLM businesses is that people at the top are frequently the winners. The vast majority of people at the bottom end up spending money and time to get involved and end up losing whatever they put in.

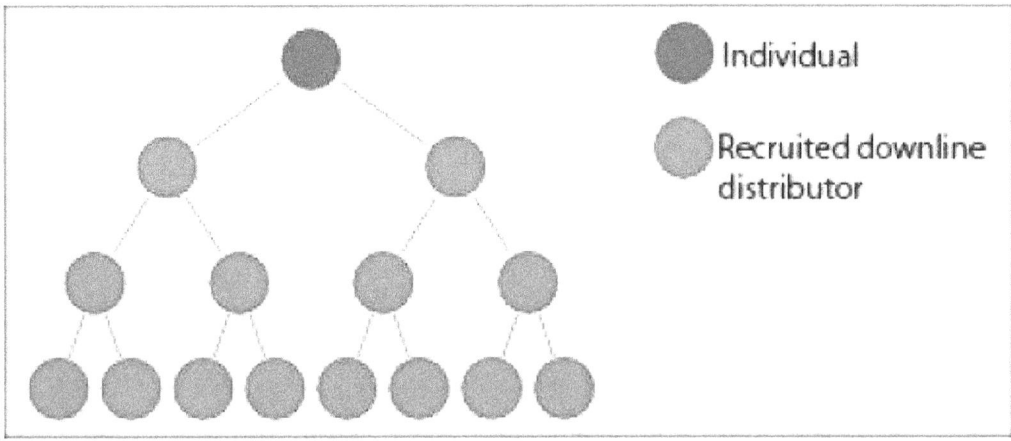

Example of a MLM business model

If you're determined to choose a business with an MLM model, be sure to check with at least a handful of other people who've entered at your level (who you identify on your own, separate from people the MLM promoter refers you to), and see what they have to say. Find out their perspectives on how - and if it's possible - to be successful.

Upside

- Typically, **limited startup costs** (a membership or initial inventory commitment).
- Viable **home-based business**.
- You are provided **pre-packaged tools, products and sales techniques**.

Downside

- **Most** people lose money in MLM activities, because they can't sell the product as effectively as they thought they could.
- Credibility can become an issue, especially if you start treating friends like they're customers.

IV. Marketing and Sales Mgmt.

1. What is your plan for marketing?
2. What is your expected growth from marketing?
3. What is your first year's sales expectations? How will you increase sales?
4. Name the other organizations/ consultants, etc. you will partner with, and how they will assist your business.
5. Is there a national network/ association you can join?
6. Will your staff need additional education to continuing education in the future to understand the market, trends, or your business, etc.?
7. Will you work with city, county, state governments?
8. Are you planning to establish a website? YouTube channel, Facebook Page, Instagram, or other social media?
9. What can people do on these sites?
10. What information will the websites provide?
11. What are some other tasks?
12. Who will perform the update to these sites and the tasks?

The State of Black Entrepreneurship

African Americans own **1.9 million businesses** in the U.S., an increase of 60.5% from 2002.

African American-owned businesses generate more than **$137.5 billion** in receipts per year. The 100 largest businesses earn more than **$19.1 billion** in revenue.

Black women are the **fastest growing** group of entrepreneurs in the U.S. - they have grown **322%** since 1997.

However,

- Only 13% of black small business owners report being able to obtain the credit they need

- African American-owned businesses account for just 7.1% of all firms

- Black business owners represent just .8% of total employment and .5% of total receipts

Source: The U.S. Census Bureau; American Express Open's 2015 State of Women-Owned Businesses Report; Wells Fargo and Gallup's Small Business Diverse Segments Lending Study.

Essential Marketing Strategies

This section is all about getting the word out about your business so customers come through your doors, or perhaps to your websites homepage, wanting to spend money on your product.

First and foremost, you'll need to study up on your target audience to develop a marketing message that will resonate with them. Are you planning on creating funny viral videos? Are you planning on utilizing YouTube to demonstrate your product or service? Are you planning on creating a Facebook page or Instagram page?

Once you've got a grasp of how to best express the product or service of what you offer, make sure you maintain that message consistently throughout your marketing efforts. It should be reinforced repeatedly to build on your brand identity, and to give people a clear reason to be interested in your business.

Below is an overview of the types of materials and a menu of marketing tactics to choose from

We touch on three essential marketing items in this step:

1. Research & Strategy
2. Marketing Materials
3. Marketing Methods

Doing Market Research & Setting a Marketing Strategy

Just as you have to do intensive research for your business plan, you should also do a healthy amount of fact-finding in order to put together a well-oiled marketing strategy. If you do, your marketing effort will be much more methodical and effective.

Who is your targeted typical buyer?

- What's a description of your target market? For example: "mothers, age 25-45, in urban locations, $90,000 household income, and college-educated."

How do your potential customers' habits and behavior play into their purchasing decisions?

- Ex: What are their "hot buttons"?
    - Specific issues with ordering from an unknown source such as
        - Time delay
        - Shipping cost
        - Credit card security concerns
    - Urgent offers, such as "This offer ends tomorrow at midnight "
    - Getting a great deal
    - Being "first" to get it (people referred to as "early adopters")
    - Being trendy (must have the latest and hottest)
    - Hand-holding and personal attention (relationships rule their pocket book)

How do you know they want your product?

- What related purchases do they make that give you confidence they'd be interested in what your product or service you offer?

How much are they willing to pay?

- You've got to figure out the all-important matter of pricing. What price tag is best for what you offer? It basically comes down to a combination of what you need to make in order to achieve workable profit margins, and what prices your customers are willing to spend. Oftentimes, it's a challenge to get these two numbers to match up. So, ask yourself:

- What's the right price, based on your costs and your estimate of the maximum amount your customers are willing to pay?
- When an item is placed on sale, will you still make a decent proit?
- What form of payment will customers want to use?
- For wholesalers, what terms of payment will they be willing to accept?
- For retailers, what profit margins can you advertise to create a great relationship between you and the store that you would like your products to be in?

Where (and how) will your customers want to buy your product or service?

- In-person or online? Via catalog or phone? From a trusted retail store or wholesaler? At a discount giant or with a high end boutique?

Why would your potential customers buy from you instead of your competition?

- This assumes your target market already demonstrates a desire to use or purchase something like what you offer. Is this so? If not, educating your customer will be critically important in your marketing. And that can be very expensive and time-consuming.
- You must know what your "value proposition" is – a crystal clear statement that anyone could understand but, most importantly, your targeted customer would quickly "get" about why they should be interested in what you offer.

What media has the greatest impact with your target market?

- Your choices are as varied today as they've ever been. There's everything from billboards at the roadside to animated online banners, from sandwich board-toting teens to direct mail through the mail slot, from online radio, Instagram, Twitter, Facebook, to cable TV, and from magazines to local classified ads. With this many options constantly coming at your prospective customer, it's more and more difficult to be sure your advertising will stand out and get the attention you want it to. Just be sure you know to what they're tuned in to so you can be confident your marketing efforts will get noticed.

Will you use basic printed material to market your business?

Have you ever entered a restaurant and ask for a menu only to find they do not have any available? What were your initial feelings for the business? Most people will answer this question with hesitation. If a restaurant is cutting corners and saving money by not printing menus, what else are they cutting corners with? Business cards, letterheads, brochures and other printed material are essential for your communication, networking and sales activities. (Remember to add these costs to your budget sheet)

1. Will you be giving these materials out to the public?
2. Will they be in your store front?
3. Will you use printed material just to promote your business to local residents for special occasions?
4. Will you printed material include coupons?
5. Do you need to create banners to advertise your store to the local community?
6. Will you place your coupons in customer mailboxes, hang them on their doors, place ads on their cars?

Grassroots Marketing

Grassroots is certainly one of the most affordable type of marketing. It consists of using resources you already have to spread the word about your product or service. Will you do any of these activities to get the word out about your product or service?

- Distribute your marketing materials (business cards, brochures, flyers) at local businesses, schools, churches and community centers.
- Give great customer service, and then ask customers to spread the word about your company and/or to write testimonials about their positive experience with your company online.
- Participate in local/community events such as festivals.
- Give donations to community organizations to Sponsor community activities in exchange for advertising your business.
- Write an article and pitch it to local papers or niche publications.
- Word-of-mouth – tell friends, family and acquaintances and ask them to tell 5 people. Talk about your business every chance you get.
- Give out free samples of your product.
- Partner with local non-profits for their cause

Networking is a great, low cost way to connect with potential customers and strategic partners to spread the news about your business. Joining your local **Chambers of Commerce** is a great way for meeting other business owners in your area. They provide an ecosystem of members who are all looking to do business, as well as provide resources for your business such as products and services at discounted prices such as office supplies, accounting services, telecommunications discounts, reduced health insurance, etc.

Trade Associations for your particular industry is another great networking resource you should consider. Often times these associations hold events, several times a year, offer industry-specific education and message boards online, and provide an opportunity for members to list their businesses on their website.

Watch TV? Do much reading? Listen to talk radio? The news that you experience comes from a combination of reporters uncovering their own story themes and pitches sent to reporters by outside sources. As a new entrepreneur with a great business fresh on the scene, you may have a highly appealing story that reporters are interested in learning and writing about. And if they do write about your business, it can be a homerun opportunity for you.

We often refer to "the power of PR," a phenomenal way to generate awareness about what you're up to--virtually for free--that will touch potentially thousands or millions of people. Many entrepreneurs say their PR efforts have benefited them in ways they could never have afforded to pay for.

The question for you should be whether you choose to do your PR in-house or, instead, use a professional firm like Rembrandt Communications, the Firm, Startup Nation etc.? There are pros and cons to both strategies.

Pros of in-house PR

- Your passion is contagious and gets the reporter's attention
- You control the message more closely

Cons of in-house PR

- You're an amateur and your pitch to reporters may seem that way
- You don't have the preexisting media contacts that a professional has

V.   Products/ Services you will provide

1. List the products/ services you will provide. Write the description for each product or service, and Include pictures of the products or services if possible. (optional)
2. What are the ingredients of the products? Is it vegan, No GMO, Certified Organic, Gluten free, paraben free, BPA free, or none of the above?
3. Do you have a logo for the products or services? Please attach to business plan if possible.
4. Who you will provide these services to?

5. Where will you concentrate your services at? (City, STATE, Zip codes, East Coast, Coast to Coast or throughout the United States.)
6. Are you planning to eventually go international with your product or service?
7. What products/ services do plan on adding to your corporate business structure in the future? Ex: If you are a beauty salon will you add nails, and make-up services? Will you add a mobile hair and make-up service?
8. What is the difference between your services and your competition? (Will you match their rate? Will your rate be lower?
9. Can you guarantee shorter transportation / delivery time?
10. Will you carry products or services the competition will not carry?
11. If transporting a product or service, Will you also provide shorter routes such as across town or carrier services that guarantees delivery that day?
12. Are you listed on Yelp, or the Yellow Pages? Do you plan on being listed to these services?
13. Will you register with the Better Business Bureau?

What's so different about what you have to offer?

To answer this question, repeat after us: research, research, and research! You can almost bet that someone's going to come up to you as you're charting a course to get into business and say, "Hey, did you know that XY Company does exactly what you do?"

If you're prepared, you'll be able to answer, "Yes, I do know, but this is how we're different." You have to be master of your domain—*the expert* in your business.

That's especially important when it comes to warming up investors and selling to customers Remember that investors will want to know why they should invest in your company rather than the guy down the street. But don't overhype your differences. Pick the ones that you can really *prove* and substantiate. It may be that one simple, but profound distinction that will be enough to create a positive effect! So don't waste time drumming up weak distinctions—rely on the strongest and lose the rest. Also, remember that the differences don't have to be rooted in a complicated technological advantage or some mysterious "secret sauce." Often, a difference stems from simply executing a product or service better than anyone else.

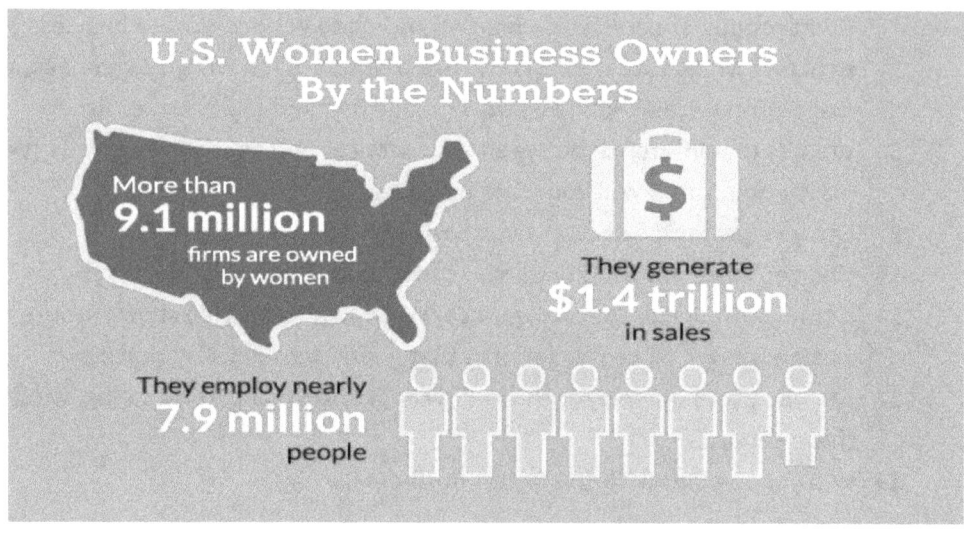

VI. <u>**Banking Relationships and Current Investors.**</u>

1. What bank do you plan on using for your business? Is the bank account currently active or are you planning on opening an account?
2. Will it be a Checking's or savings, or both?
3. Why did you choose this bank?
4. What services can they provide for your business?
5. Are they local or a national bank?
6. Do you have any current investors?
7. How much have you personally invested in the business? What has been some of the things you have accomplished to get this business started?
8. Do you have a current social media presence established online pertaining to your business? Are you actively speaking with others about your business idea?
9. How will you raise money for the start-up costs?
10. Will you raise money by selling stock certificates?
11. Do you own the entire company or do you have other partners?

VII. Financials

1. Do you have any assets to borrow against? (Most banks and SBA will require assets you can borrow against / or put up as collateral). (Equipment, Coins, diamonds, IRA, stocks, bonds, Mutual Funds, anything of value that can be sold or liquidated can be considered.)
2. If so, list them and their appraised value. Attach an appraisal letter or form if available.
3. Will you need a financial loan to get started? Or can you start the business with a website and other basic necessities?
4. Have you incorporated your business with your State Business Services Office (Secretary of State already? If not what are the costs? If so, include your incorporation certificate.
5. How much money does the business have currently in its bank account?
6. Will you need to purchase industrial equipment? Office Equipment?
7. How much more money will you need in the next year, three years and five years?
8. Will the money you are seeking will be used for salaries for your workers? To invest in the product/ service? Etc. Explain.
9. Will the money you are seeking be used to improve upon your existing product or service?
10. Will you need a manufacturer or distributor for you product? Have you already secured a manufacturer or distributor to help you in this business? If not, do you have a list of potential companies you are inquiring to?
11. Have you researched the average costs to produce this product or service?
12. What will be the wholesale and retail rate be per produced unit? Case?
13. Do you have a minimum ordering requirement or wholesalers / retailers?
14. For a service, what will your discounted group rate be as well as the retail rate?
15. Will you be receiving funding from grants or business loans? (Have you already applied for loans or grants in the past 12 months?)
16. Do you have any loans that that you have already accepted and is paying on currently?
17. Are these loans in good standing?
18. Do you have any credit cards in the business name? What do you use your credit cards for?

19. How much do you need in start-up costs? Explain the amount and (Also attach your budget sheet)
20. When do you expect to open your doors for business? Listing Month and Year is fine.
21. Are your operating the business now?
22. Do you have any business accounts already established? Sam's Club, Staples, Office Maxx, Wholesalers, Do you have Any services that you have already established.
From which companies?
How long have they been in existence or how old is the account?

***If you do not have any accounts in your business name, you can work on acquiring these accounts by applying for accounts that are easy to establish. Some of the easiest places to establish a business account:

1. Amazon Business Account
2. Costco, or Sam's Club membership
3. USPS Post Office online for correspondence and discounts or shipping or
4. UPS / FED Ex for discounts for volume shipping for business owners
5. Yelp or Yellow Pages for general contact information and the location of your business.
6. Facebook to speak with customers, advertising, and to announce sales.
7. Office Depot, Office Maxx, Staples, or Quill.com for office supplies and office equipment.
8. Phone Service or answering service (If you do not have a physical location for your business, but you need to speak to customers or investors) Ring Central is a great service that you can utilize.
9. Switch phone and / or internet service to business name
10. Create a website (Shopify, Squarespace, Web.com, or Weebly are the most popular for most businesses

Other ways to look for Financing

Are you seeking an Angel Investor?

Angel investors are individuals who invest in companies at an early stage in exchange for equity and the chance to help guide the company. In contrast, venture capitalists invest as a profession and generally on behalf of other investors.

Generally one is ready to approach angels when they have exhausted their friends and family but are not yet ready to approach venture capitalists for money.

Approach angels if you are looking for large amounts ($25K to $1M) of "smart money" - the people who provide this form of funding have already "made it big" in their own careers and can help guide you to do the same.

Upside

- Angels invest more than money - they provide mentoring and contacts.
- Angels are patient about their investment.
- There are no monthly payments with this type of financing - angels make their money when you achieve your business exit strategy.

Downside

- Angels are difficult to find.
- Angels deserve regular and thorough reporting, which can take up valuable time.
- You are giving up equity in your company.

1. Factoring

Factoring is where the financial institution (factor) advances the entrepreneur money against proceeds from the entrepreneur's outstanding accounts receivables. Factoring firms generally are paid a percentage of the invoice's value.

2. Venture Capitalists

Venture capitalists are individuals or companies with large amounts of capital to invest and expect higher returns.

Use Venture Capitalists if you already have a great track record in your field or as an entrepreneur, and if you have a business concept that will require a lot of money ($250K to $10s of millions) and will have a rapid growth curve.

Upside

- VCs invest smarts and networking, in addition to money.
- VCs typically have more money available if you need it to grow down the road.

Downside

- VCs typically only invest in established companies.
- You must be willing to give up significant control over major decisions for your company.
- You must have a "fast growth" company.
- You must have an aggressive exit strategy to sell your business or do an IPO within 5-7 years.

3. Funding from your church members (will also be included in this section)

VIII. Summary of Company Growth and Market highlights

1. What have you been doing since the company began?
2. Has the company grown? Are you or will you be the first to combine these services for your industry?
3. What is the yearly expected growth for your business? And the industry in general
4. How do you plan on measuring your growth?
5. Will you use an independent firm to assist you in measuring your growth?
6. How big is the business in the United States and Internationally?
7. What products are typically used for your product or service? How have you secured these products or services from other vendors or manufacturers?
8. Is there a season(s) of the year where your business is more profitable?
9. What season is it not as profitable?
10. What is your SWOT (strengths, weaknesses, opportunities, and threats to your business and the market that you are getting into?)
11. How will you contact your customers to see what their opinion is of your product or service?
12. If there is a complaint about your business or product, who will handle the issue? Explain the process
13. How will you constantly improve upon the product or service?
14. How will you let your customers know about improvements?

How will you measure success?

For so many people, money made is the big measurement of success. But while financial achievements will be fundamental to your business's viability, there's more to gain from running a business than just making money. It's important to define what success means to you, as we discussed in Chapter Three. We measure success which keeps us grounded in our ideas of work as freedom, work as family, and work as fulfillment. What will yours be? As part of the business-planning process, consider how you'll define success.

IX. Summary of Management and Future plans

1. How will you plan to manage your business? Why did you choose this management model?
2. What goals will you set for your business at the first, third and fifth year?
3. How many customers do you plan to service the first, third, and fifth year?
4. What are your key milestones? Create a chart that shows dates when you expect to achieve key milestones as your business launches and grows.
5. How do you plan on mitigating market loss?
   What happens when a cheaper competitor provides the same product or service?
6. Is your product popular now but in a year may be unpopular? Does it have longevity? If not, what other products are you going to introduce?
7. How are you planning to deal with job downsizing layoffs/ or loss?
8. How are you planning on dealing with transportation, shipping or gas increases?
9. How are you planning on dealing with other threats that may affect your business?
10. What are some of your future plans for your business?
11. If this plan does not work out what is your plan B, plan C, and plan D. How can you look at the business in another way, and utilize your skills to change the business to make it successful?
12. If you have more than one business or DBA, List the divisions of your business and the summaries of their objectives.

Visual Map

It is very helpful to have a visual map of what has to happen *and when* to keep you focused on your priorities. While many times your guesstimates of a major milestone will be off the mark, those milestones are important because they'll keep you accountable as you evaluate your progress. If you're not hitting your key milestones, it'll force you to get real about your performance, your resources, and the resolve you'll need to get back on track. You may decide that a "plan B" shift in thinking is required. But without the milestone chart, you'll never know if you need to shift or respond until it's way too late.

Your vision should not be contingent upon one person to carry the load for the entire company. What if that person is sickly, unable to make it to the meetings, or god forbid dies? The company will be left in a sea of chaos, as other partners figure out what to do to carry on the business, and without any direction, most businesses will likely suffer. This is a very common result of one person, holding the load, or being the go to person for everything relating to company business, and everyone else takes orders from this one person.

If you have a small office, group of people, or partners working with you, creating a plan, or visual map can be a great exercise to do together, to ensure each of your team members are on the same page as to where they see the business going, and how we can all arrive at the end goal together. Although it may be difficult to get others to see your dream as you do, your team members may have other ideas that you can implement in your own plans, which will work for the benefit of the entire company. As a business, try to create a visual map of where you see the company going, and what other revenue streams you can add onto the business for the next three, five, and ten years. The plans may change, and may need to be altered over time however, at least you will have a rough draft of future plans, just in case anything happens.

Goals

Stay focused. Many wealthy persons attribute their success to creating a goals list. I prefer to create a weekly, monthly, and yearly goals list so I am constantly working towards a goal each week. If you do not finish your goals list, carry over the things to accomplish, or things to do for the next week, so that you can finish the list before the month ends.

At the end of the month, I look over each week's list, to ensure I have not missed any steps when accomplishing my goals, and I write a new list or Main Goal for the next month.

At the end of the year, I reflect on my years' worth of writings, and look to see if I had accomplished my goals for the year.

Example, if I want to set a goal to write at least twelve new books for children during the year, and each book specializes on a particular subject. I know that means I need to create, write, and publish a book at least once a month. Although some subjects require research, and to contract the services out to others, my goals has not changed because I have one month to finish this goal. At the end of the year, I project that my sales for each book will be at least $1,000 so I can measure my success based upon the demand of the book, and knowing that I have completed 12 new books for the year.

Visit your local Office supply store to get a goals book, or simply write down in a notebook your weekly, monthly, and yearly goals. Then get started by thinking about what you need to do to carry out each of these goals in a month, followed by carrying out these tasks each week.

X. Appendix

Attach the following information at the end of your completed business plan document.

1. Include your resume for yourself and all of your officers.
2. It will include letters and /or statements from your existing credit accounts in good standing and personal financial information if possible.
3. A copy of your incorporation documents
4. A copy of licenses, permits, and DBA documents, if applicable.
5. Credit report if requested. (Some banks or funding sources will ask for a copy of your credit report. It will be listed in this section of the business plan.)
6. Contact information and/or company profile of accountants or an accounting firm you wish to hire.
7. Consultants with consultant profile and contact information you plan on using for your business
8. Will you be hiring a payroll service such as ADP? Who did you contact at ADP, and what is their contact information?
9. If you are a non-profit, include letters of support from existing established nonprofits will be attached to the business plan in this section.

10. Historical financial statements if it's an existing business
11. Previous tax returns for at least three years
12. Reference letters from business associates and partners
13. Personal financial statements, and or tax returns
14. Facilities Diagram, if you do not currently have a physical place of business currently.
15. Existing contracts
16. Purchase orders, if applicable
17. Letters of Intent, if applicable
18. Budget Sheets
19. Business loan application

Budget sheet Considerations

Are you confused over how much money you'll need for your startup business? There's an easy approach to breaking this mystery down and creating a clear plan for the funds that your startup business will need.

Keep in mind that different small businesses will have different types of startup costs. For example, a furniture retailer might need a storefront and staff to maintain its business. While a toy manufacturer might need manufacturing equipment, a warehouse and staff that is trained to operate the equipment. If you're operating an online retail business, you might be doing it at home in your PJs, and don't need a facility or staff at all.

Costs for a startup business can be divvied up into six major categories:

- **Cost of sales**: Product inventory, raw materials, manufacturing equipment, shipping, packaging, shipping insurance, warehousing, transaction fees for credit card and debit cards.
- **Professional fees**: Setting up a legal structure for your business (e.g. LLC, corporation), trademarks, copyrights, patents, drafting partnership and non-disclosure agreements, attorney fees for ongoing consultation, retaining an accountant, freelancers, contract

workers, Payroll services. Real Estate Agent fees, cost of real estate, and real estate closing costs.
- **Technology costs:** Computer hardware, computer software, printers, cell phones, PDAs, website development and maintenance, website hosting fees, high-speed internet access, servers, security measures, IT consulting, tablets, laptops, etc.
- **Administrative costs:** Various types of business insurance, office supplies, licenses and permits, express shipping and postage, product packaging, parking, rent, utilities, phones, copier, fax machine, desks, chairs, filing cabinets – anything else you need to have on a daily basis to operate a business, car rental fees, equipment rental fees, Traveling fees (airplane, hotel gas mileage reimbursements, and other accommodations. Club membership yearly fees (Costco etc.) Office décor and decorations fees
- **Sales and marketing costs:** Printing of stationery, marketing materials, advertising, public relations, event or trade show attendance or sponsorship, trade association or chamber of commerce membership fees, travel and entertainment for client meetings, mailing or lead lists , Yelp BBB, flyers, banners, business cards, Social media Advertising,
- **Wages and benefits**: Employee salaries, payroll taxes, workers compensation, insurance, (medical, dental, supplemental health or none) Include the cost of living adjustment for each of your employees. You will certainly value the people helping to make your business a successful one. When will you expect to repay them for their loyalty by offering them a raise? Every year, three years or five years? What will the percentage of the raise be?

When doing the research for your business costs, use the median cost on your budget sheet. Do not list the most expensive product you need in your business model, nor should you list the cheapest. Investors know the average cost for products and services, especially if they are used to looking at budget sheets for businesses all the time. You do not want to project the image of someone who spends a tremendous amount of money on the best of products/ supplies and cannot justify why you are paying a higher price for this product or supply. Business costs change, and so does the cost for supplies. Listing a median cost will give you some room to adjust the price as you look for a better quality product or ingredient without costing more money.

List everything down to the expected Electric Bill for a large facility. If you are unsure what the cost of the facility electric expense is, you can call the electric company, and ask them, what is the average cost of the electric / water at the address of the building that is similar to the one you will need?

Decorating ideas is something overlooked but necessary when it comes to making the facility look presentable and used as a teaching tool. Markers and crayons, paint, etc. Will these supplies need to be replaced on a monthly basis? Literally every cent you spend to get the business going must be accounted for.

This can be achieved by saving your receipts, keeping a record of what you are spending, including the fees to incorporate, to file a DBA, fees to hire a business consultant , everything in relation to you putting money out for your business will be a write off for you during tax season.

Additional templates and assistance

Some Banks will offer Small Business / Entrepreneurship classes to help those clients who are seeking funding from their bank, get financed prior to applying and being denied. This is a great way to learn about what banks are looking for when reviewing business proposals.

Although there are some outstanding programs your city may offer to help small business entrepreneurs get started, especially with your local Chamber of Commerce, and local Community College, there are other good resources we can utilize online as well. We recommend the website www.score.org to assist you in creating your business proposal budget.

They have several templates listed on their website, (mostly in Excel format), where the user can type the numbers on the provided spreadsheet, and the template formats your data for you. Some of these templates found on SCORE are:

SCORE Financial Projections Template	Start-Up Expenses
Opening Day Balance Sheet	Balance Sheet (Projected)
Bank Loan Request for Small Business	Loan Amortization Schedule
Break-Even Analysis	12-Month Cash Flow Statement
3-Year Cash Flow Statement	Financial History & Ratios
Personal Financial Statement	12-Month Profit and Loss Projection
3-Year Profit and Loss Projection	Marketing & Sales Templates
Sales Forecast (12 Months)	Marketing Plan Guide
Product and Service Description Worksheet	Target Market Data Worksheet
Target Market Comparison Worksheet	Competitive Data Collection Plan
Competitive Analysis Worksheet	Brand Message Worksheet
Pricing Strategy Worksheet	Distribution Channel Assessment Worksheet
Marketing Expenses Strategy Chart	Annual Marketing Budget Template
Marketing Calendar Template	Management Templates
Job Analysis Worksheet	

Final thoughts

Although, it may seem like a business plan is a tremendous task to take on for an individual, it is not. We hope that we've given you great advice throughout this process which will allow you to write the perfect business plan to acquire the funding you need.

Our first book in the series of Business Planning focused on jobs, contracts, and odd ways you can earn a living by utilizing the internet. The jobs listed in the book, "The Housewives Guide to becoming wealthy by Working at home" gave readers a tremendous amount of information needed to earn an income if necessary, by the end of the day, in most cases, the end of the week, through contracts that did not require a business license.

Our next few books in this series will be Business Contracts, whereby we teach new businesses how to write, fill out and submit contracts for jobs, as well as acquire new relationships by hiring consultants through writing contracts. This is a great resource of you are just getting started and you do not have the expertise to get your business where it needs to be, and you want to outsource assistance from others. This book is also great for someone wanting to do business contracts directly with other companies by providing a service to them, or the general public.

The follow up book in this series will focus more on Incorporation process and how to establish the correct Corporation for your business. Most people will read this information, and be amazed at the background of Corporations in America because of its original origins. Other's may read the information, and become completely shocked out of establishing a business.

Nevertheless, it is important to understand what you are doing when we incorporate a business so that we can use the business structure to our best advantage.

Remember that we are wanting to establish a business to make additional income for ourselves and control our own destiny. This is a privilege that is given to most Americans, but is rarely given to the general public in many countries around the world.

Having a very diverse background of people from all walks of life will enhance any business, because all cultures have a different perception of the world in which we live in. Different cultures can reach different customers thereby making your business a multi-national company, not just a company based in one country with no way to grow your business to a international level.

The best advice we can give you is from the beginning of your corporations' formation, make plans for your business to fail. Failing is a natural occurrence when you are just entering the market for the first time, as it will be a learning lesson for you. That is why it is so important to learn from your mistakes, and take the knowledge that you acquire to try again.

Practice makes perfect. Just like the nursery rhyme the Tortoise and the Hare; we cannot not all be a sprinting hare that has the strength, stamina, and hopping skills in the beginning of a race. The slow, and consistent movements, checking our work three times if necessary, will be the pace we should go for when planning and executing a product relating to business.

Remember that market uncertainties can affect the bottom line of your business. We cannot foresee a Tsunami that will hit the Asian cost, which will wipe out suppliers for the next six months, nor can we predict that our President may enact Tariff (or extreme taxes) on goods produced and imported into our country. Make plans to make over the three times your cost, also known as the Winning Formula for your business so that you can earn the additional money you need to stay in business, when everyone else may be going out of business for good.

Ten Ways to Ruin Your Business Plan

These errors in business plan preparation and presentation will undermine the

Credibility of the plan and hurt your chances to receive funding:

- • Submitting a "rough copy," (with coffee stains and typos) tells the reader that Management doesn't take the planning process seriously.
- • Outdated historical financial information or unrealistic industry comparisons will leave doubts about the entrepreneur's planning abilities.
- • Unsubstantiated assumptions can hurt a business plan; the business owner must be prepared to explain the "why" of every point in the plan.
- • Too much "blue sky" - a failure to consider prospective pitfalls - will lead the reader to conclude that the idea is not realistic.
- • A lack of understanding of financial information. Even if someone else prepares the projections, the owner must be able to explain them.
- • Lack of specific, detailed strategies. A plan that includes only general statements of strategy ("We will provide world class service and the lowest possible price.") Without important details will be dismissed as fluff.

Especially important if the business plan is prepared for a lender:

- • No indication that the owner has anything at stake. The lender expects the entrepreneur to have some equity capital invested in the business.
- • Unwillingness to personally guarantee any loans. If the business owner isn't willing to stand behind his or her company, then why should the bank?
- • Starting the plan with unrealistic loan amounts or terms. Do your homework and propose a realistic structure.
- • Too much focus on collateral. Even for a cash-secured loan, the banker is looking toward projected profits for repayment of the loan. Cash flow should be emphasized as the source of repayment. looking toward projected profits for repayment of the loan.

Loan Proposal Outline

The following items should be provided to the lender with your loan request. Incomplete or inadequate information will result in delays. Please *do not* condense information at the expense of clarity.

1. **Description of Business:** Provide a written description of your business including information about:

   A. Type of organization
   B. Date of information
   C. Location
   D. Product or service
   E. Brief history
   F. Proposed Future Operation
   G. Competition
   H. Customers
   I. Suppliers

2. **Management Experience:** Resumes of each owner and key management members.

3. **Personal Financial Statements:** Financial statements are required of all principal owners (20% or more) and guarantors. Financial statements should not be older than 90 days. Please attach a copy of last years federal income tax return to the financial statement.

4. **Loan Repayment:** Provide a brief written statement indicating how the loan will be repaid, including repayment sources and time requirements. This statement should be supported by cash-flow schedules, budgets, and other appropriate information.

   A. **Existing Business:** Provide at least the past 3 years financial statements, plus a current dated statement (no older than 90 days) to include balance sheets and profit & loss statements. Agings of accounts payable and accounts receivables should be included, as well as, a schedule of term debt.

   B. **Proposed Business:** Please provide a pro-forma balance sheet reflecting sources and uses of *both* equity and borrowed funds.

   C. **Projections:** Please provide a projection of future operations for at least 3 years. How much money you expect to take in; what expenses will be; and on what you base these estimates. The projections should be in profit & loss format. Explain assumptions used (if different from trend or industry standards).

5. **Other Items as they Apply:**

   Leases (copies of proposal)
   Franchise Agreement
   Purchase Agreement
   Articles of Incorporation
   Plans, Specifications
   Copies of Licenses
   Letters of reference
   Letters of Intent
   Contracts
   Partnership Agreement

6. **List Collateral:** Real property and other assets to be held as collateral.

Sample - Business Proposal Letter
DATE

ABC Global Advertising
12678 Nancy Wilson Way
Chillicothe, Ohio 45601

Attn: Caroline Smith

Dear Ms. Smith,

Are you tired of spending the company's money trying to gather new leads each week? We know how hard it can be to make cold calls and come up with little to no interest. Like any growing business, you need solid leads to work from each week. Because you are a national advertising agency, you have a big opportunity to branch out and make bigger money.

Lead Smart has been helping companies like yours for over 10 years get the leads they need. We too are a nationwide company and can provide your business with good leads. This permits business to stop using ineffective methods that include cold calls. Our leads are 100% generated from internet questionnaires that companies have responded too. These are potential customers who have specified they have a need of your type of services and want to hear from your company.

Our company has employees who have been here since the day we opened. Our workers are knowledgeable and are willing to go the extra mile for our customers. We don't just hire anybody to handle our business. We selected the best of the best to service our customers. At Lead Smart, we understand that you're not just a number and you will always get the best customer service around.

If you are tired of scrounging for leads for new business and need help, we are the ones to call. Our fresh leads and pulled right from the internet on a daily basis. Call today to see how we can save you money and generate new business.

Sincerely,

Tom Evans

President of Lead Smart

Sample - Business Proposal Letter
DATE

ABC Marketing Experts
443 Anywhere Drive
Rockford, IL 61101
Attn: Mr. Ben Smith

Dear Mr. Ben Smith,

Are you looking for a new and better way to spend your company's resources on gathering new business leads every week? Our organization understands how difficult and frustrating it is to make numerous cold calls day after day that lead to very little interest overall. Every thriving business needs solid leads each and every week in order to survive and grow. Since you are such a high-profile marketing agency, you have a golden opportunity to expand and reap bigger profits.

New Leads, Inc. has been assisting companies and other organization like yours for more than 8 years. Our company enables businesses to stop implementing unsuccessful methods like cold calling or direct mailing in order to gain new leads. Our solid leads are derived from Internet questionnaires that certain companies have already responded to and are interested in. Basically, these are potential clients who have specifically shown a keen interest in your products or services and are simply waiting for you to contact them.

Our experienced staff is quite knowledgeable and always goes the extra mile on behalf of our customers. We are very selective about who we hire to handle our business, which is why we've chosen only the finest people available to work for our organization in order to best serve our clients. At New Leads, Inc., we know how valuable you are to the livelihood of our own organization and therefore take your needs and concerns very seriously. Great customer service is our top priority.

If you're fed up of begging for leads that will potentially boost your business, New Leads, Inc. is here to help. Our leads are fresh and come straight from the Internet every day. Contact us today to take your business to a whole new level while saving a great deal of money along the way.

Sincerely,

(sign your name here)

Thomas Smart
CEO of New Leads, Inc

Sample - Business Proposal Letter

Name of Sender
Name of Sender's Plumbing Company
Address of Company
City, State, Zip Code

DATE

Name of Building Manager or Owner
Address of Manager or Owner
City, State, Zip Code

RE: Apartment Complex Plumbing Services

Dear Name of Manager or Owner,

This letter is intended to formally propose plumbing services for the Name of Apartment Complex. We have been successfully maintaining the plumbing systems in more than 10 apartment complexes in CITY, for the past 25 years and would be happy to give testimonials from our customers. We respond 24/7 to all emergency requirements and make sure the plumbing in every apartment is working efficiently.

A service maintenance contract from us offers a significant savings compared to calling a plumber every time there is a problem. It also takes the responsibility from your shoulders. We give you a 90 day guarantee on repairs and new installations for parts and labor.

I have included a copy of the standard contract that gives an estimate for the cost. However, it can be modified to your specific requirements. I would be happy to talk to you about our services and answer any questions. I can be reached at [555-123-4567] or at [Name@email.com].

Sincerely,

Signature of Plumbing Contractor
Printed Name of Plumbing Contractor
List of Enclosures: copy of standard contract

Sample - Business Partnership Letter

COMPANY LETTERHEAD IF APPLICABLE
Name of Sender
Name of Sender's Business if applicable
Address of Sender
City, State, Zip Code

DATE

Name of Receiver
Name of Receiver's Business if applicable
Address of Receiver
City, State, Zip Code

Dear Name of Receiver,

This is a Letter of Intent that proposes to outline the partnership you and I discussed on DATE. I do not consider the terms and conditions stated in this letter as binding and am open to negotiation.

We have agreed that we will enter into partnership for the purposes of starting a catering service. My main responsibility will be food preparation and purchasing, and your responsibility will be accounts and marketing. We will pay ourselves and our employees a suitable salary and split any profits after salaries 50-50. We are still negotiating the amount of salaries.

We have also agreed to take out a Small Business Loan to cover the start-up expenses and will both be signatory for that loan. We have together created a business plan that clearly states our intentions for the short-term as well as the next five years, and this plan has been approved by the bank.

I propose we meet in two weeks on DATE at the office of Name of Lawyer to confirm the salaries and sign a contract of partnership. We can meet at a time of your convenience to discuss the points on which we have not yet agreed before we meet the lawyer. Please call me at 555-123-4567 or contact me at Name@email.com to set up a meeting.

This letter is a formal expression of intent to start a partnership with you to open a catering service. We need to decide the main points of financial distribution and meet the lawyer to sign the contract.

Sincerely,

Signature of Sender
Printed Name of Sender

Sample - Business Plan for IT Company

Executive Summary

IT-Advisers will be formed as a consulting company specializing in marketing of information technology and hi-tech products in international markets. Its founders are former marketers of consulting services, cloud-based software and market research, all in international markets.

They are founding IT-Advisers to formalize the consulting services they offer.

Mission

IT Advisers (ITA) offers high-tech manufacturers and IT-companies a reliable, high quality alternative to in-house resources for business development, market research and channel development on an international scale.

A true alternative to in house resources offers a very high level of practical experience, know how, contacts and confidentiality. Clients must know that working with ITA is a more professional, less risky way to develop new areas even than working completely in house with their own people. ITA must also be able to maintain financial balance, charging a high value for its services and delivering an even higher value to its clients. Initial focus will be development in the European and Latin American markets, or for European clients in the United States market.

Keys to Success

1. Excellence in fulfilling the promise completely confidential, reliable, trustworthy expertise and information.

2. Developing visibility to generate new business leads.

3. Leveraging from a single pool of expertise into multiple revenue generation opportunities: retainer consulting, project consulting, market research, and market research published reports.

Main financial measures

	2012	2013	2014
Cash	3,422	52,939	114,404

Sales revenue	1,175,000	1,800,000	2,450,000
Net profit for financial year	-112,509	76,547	210,178
Operating margin	-9.58%	4.25%	8.58%
Owners' equity	22,491	159,038	349,216
Return on equity (per year)	-500%	48.1%	60.2%

Company Overview

IT Advisers (ITA) is a new company providing high-level expertise in international high-tech business development, channel development, distribution strategies and marketing of high tech products. It will focus initially on providing two kinds of international triangles:

1. Providing United States clients with development for European and Latin American markets.

2. Providing United Kingdom and European clients with development for the US and Latin American markets.

As it grows it will take on people and consulting work in related markets, such as the rest of Latin America and the Far East, also similar markets. As it grows it will look for additional leverage by taking brokerage positions and representation positions to create percentage holdings in product results.

ITA will be created as a California C corporation based in San Jose, owned by its principal investors and principal operators. As of this writing it has not been chartered yet and is still considering alternatives of legal formation. The initial office will be established in a quality office space in the "Silicon Valley" area of California, the heart of the U.S. high tech and software industry.

ITA offers expertise in channel distribution, channel development, software and market development, sold and packaged in various ways that allow clients to choose their preferred relationship: these include small business consulting relationships, project based consulting, relationship and alliance brokering, sales representation and market representation, project based market research, published market research and information forum events.

Pic 1. ITA Headquarters

Products and Services

ITA offers the expertise a IT-company needs to develop new product distribution and new market segments in new markets. This can be taken as high-level retainer consulting, market research reports, software applications and/or project-based consulting.

Retainer consulting - we represent a client company as an extension of its business development and market development functions. This begins with complete understanding of the client company's situation, objectives, business plan, and constraints. We then represent the client company quietly and confidentially, sifting through new market developments and new opportunities as is appropriate to the client, representing the client in initial talks with possible allies, vendors and channels.

Project consulting - Proposed and billed on a per-project and per- milestone basis, project consulting offers a client company a way to harness our specific qualities and use our expertise to solve specific problems, develop and write business plans, develop specific information, software.

Market research - group studies available to selected clients at $5,000 per unit. A group study is packaged and published, a complete study of a specific market, channel, or topic. Examples might be studies of developing consumer channels in Brazil or Mexico, or implications of changing margins in software.

In the future ITA will broaden the coverage by expanding into coverage of additional markets (e.g. all of Latin America, Far East, Western Europe) and additional product areas (e.g. telecommunications, web-based software and technology integration). We are also studying the possibility of newsletter or electronic newsletter services, or perhaps special on- topic reports.

Pricing and Sales

ITA (IT-Advisers) will be priced at the upper edge of what the market will bear, competing with the name brand consultants.

Consulting should be based on $5,000 per day for project consulting, $2,000 per day for market research, and $10,000 per month and up for retainer consulting. Market research reports should be priced at $5,000 per report, which will of course require that reports be very well planned, focused on very important topics very well presented.

The annual sales projections, gross margins and cost of sales are included here in the following tables.

Products and services	Sales revenue (USD)		
	2012	2013	2014
Retainer Consulting	400,000	650,000	1,000,000
Project Consulting	500,000	750,000	900,000
Market Research	200,000	300,000	400,000
Strategic Reports and Software	75,000	100,000	150,000
	1,175,000	1,800,000	2,450,000

Products and services	Gross margin (%)		
	2012	2013	2014

Products and services			
Retainer Consulting	85	85	85
Project Consulting	85	85	85
Market Research	30	30	30
Strategic Reports and Software	70	70	70

Cost of sales (USD)

Products and services	2012	2013	2014
Retainer Consulting	60,000	97,500	150,000
Project Consulting	75,000	112,500	135,000
Market Research	140,000	210,000	280,000
Strategic Reports and Software	22,500	30,000	45,000
	297,500	450,000	610,000

Break-even analysis (USD)

	2012	2013	2014
Sales revenue	1,175,000	1,800,000	2,450,000
Cost of sales	297,500	450,000	610,000
Variable expenses, total	297,500	450,000	610,000
Labor cost	727,260	897,000	1,110,900
Other operating expenses	265,000	322,500	455,000
Depreciation of fixed assets	5,000	15,000	15,000
Financial expenses	5,250	30,448	25,569
Fixed expenses, total	1,002,510	1,264,948	1,606,469
Gross margin	74.7%	75%	75.1%

Break-even sales revenue	1,342,391	1,686,597	2,139,049
Sales revenue above break-even	0	113,403	310,951

Marketing Strategy

ITA will be focusing on information technology manufacturers of computer hardware and software, services, networking, who want to sell into markets in the United States, United Kingdom, Europe, and Latin America. These are mostly larger companies, and occasionally medium-sized companies.

Our most important group of potential customers are executives in larger corporations. These are marketing managers, general managers, sales managers, sometimes charged with international focus and sometimes charged with market or even specific channel focus. They do not want to waste their time or risk their money looking for bargain information or questionable expertise. As they go into markets looking at new opportunities, they are very sensitive to risking their company's name and reputation.

The consulting industry is pulverized and disorganized, thousands of smaller consulting organizations and individual consultants for every one of the few dozen well-known companies. Consulting is a disorganized industry, with participants ranging from major international name brand consultants to tens of thousands of individuals. One of ITA's challenges will be establishing itself as a "real" consulting company, positioned as a relatively risk free corporate purchase.

At the highest level are the few well established major names in management consulting.

Most of these are organized as partnerships established in major markets around the world, linked together by interconnecting directors and sharing the name and corporate wisdom.

Some evolved from accounting companies and some from management consulting. These companies charge very high rates for consulting and maintain relatively high overhead structures and fulfillment structures based on partners selling and junior associates fulfilling.

At the intermediate level are some function specific or market specific consultants, such as the market research firms or channel development firms.

Market segmentation

☐ Large manufacturer corporations - our most important market segment is the large manufacturer of high-technology products, such as Apple, Hewlett-Packard, IBM, Microsoft. These companies will be calling on ITA for development functions that are better spun off than managed in-house, and for market research, and for market forums.

☐ Medium sized growth companies: particularly in software, multimedia, and some related high growth fields, ITA will be able to offer an attractive development alternative to the company that is management constrained and unable to address opportunities in new markets and new market segments.

Competition

The competition comes in several forms:

1. The most significant competition is no consulting at all, companies choosing to do business development, planning and channel development and market research in house.

Their own managers do this on their own, as part of their regular business

Functions. Our key advantage in competition with in-house development is that managers are already overloaded with responsibilities, they don't have time for additional responsibilities in new market development or new channel development.

Also, ITA can approach alliances, vendors, and channels on a confidential basis, gathering information and making initial contacts in ways that the corporate managers can't.

2. The high-level prestige management consulting: McKinsey, Boston Consulting Group, etc. These are essentially generalists who take their name-brand management consulting into specialty areas. Their other very important weakness is the management structure that has the partners selling new jobs, and inexperienced associates delivering the work. We compete against them as experts in our specific fields, and with the guarantee that our clients will have the top-level people doing the actual work.

3. The third general kind of competitor is the international market research company:

Dataquest, Stanford Research Institute, etc. These companies are formidable competitors for published market research and market forums, but cannot provide the kind of high-level consulting that ITA will provide.

4. The fourth kind of competition is the market-specific smaller house. For example:

Nomura Research in Japan.

5. Sales representation, brokering and deal catalysts are an ad-hoc business form that will be defined in detail by the specific nature of each individual case.

Management and Staffing

The initial management team depends on the founders themselves, with little back-up. As we grow we will take on additional consulting help, plus graphic/editorial, sales, and marketing.

ITA should be mainly managed by working partners. In the beginning we assume 3-5 partners. We will invite one international partner from Europe. The organization has to be very flat in the beginning, with each of the founders responsible for his or her own work and management.

The ITA business requires a very high level of international experience and expertise, which means that it will not be easily leveraged in the common consulting company mode in which partners run the business and make sales, while associates fulfill. Partners will necessarily be involved in the fulfillment of the core business proposition, providing the expertise to the clients.

The initial personnel plan is still tentative. It should involve 3-5 partners, 1-3 consultants, 1 strong marketing person, an office manager. Later we add more partners, consultants and sales staff.

The annual personal estimates are included in the tables presented below.

Personnel	**Headcount**		
	2012	2013	2014
Partners	4	5	7
Consultants	4	4	4

Marketing manager	0	1	1
Sales reps	2	2	2
Office manager	1	1	1

	Average monthly salary (USD)		
Personnel	2012	2013	2014
Partners	5,200	5,500	6,000
Consultants	5,100	5,200	5,300
Marketing manager	4,600	4,700	4,800
Sales reps	4,200	4,400	4,600
Office manager	3,100	3,200	3,300

	Labor cost (USD)		
	2012	2013	2014
Wages and salaries	632,400	780,000	966,000
Social security costs	94,860	117,000	144,900
Labor cost	727,260	897,000	1,110,900
REVENUES	1,175,000	1,800,000	2,450,000
Labor cost to revenues	61.9%	49.8%	45.3%

Implementation

Total start-up expense (including legal costs, branding, stationery, other one-time expenses) come to $30,000. The annual overhead expense estimates are presented in the table below.

Start-up assets required include $50,000 in fixed assets like office furniture, computers, software and other equipment and tools.

Other operating expenses (USD)

Other operating expenses	2012	2013	2014
Startup expenses	30,000	0	0
Marketing	50,000	60,000	70,000
Travel	100,000	150,000	250,000
Office expenses and software costs	75,000	100,000	120,000
Insurance	5,000	5,000	5,000
Other fixed expenses	5,000	7,500	10,000

Assets purchase value (USD)

Fixed assets	2012	2013	2014
Startup fixed assets (equipment)	50,000	0	0
New office	0	500,000	0

Financial Projections

The paid-in capital from partners and other investors will be $135,000.

An annuity loan will be taken from a bank in amount of $500,000 for 60 months.

The performance measures, business plan financial projections and break-even analysis are presented below.

Performance measures (USD)

	2012	2013	2014
Sales revenue	1,175,000	1,800,000	2,450,000
Cost of sales	297,500	450,000	610,000
Gross profit	877,500	1,350,000	1,840,000

Other operating expenses	265,000	322,500	455,000
Labor cost	727,260	897,000	1,110,900
Depreciation of fixed assets	5,000	15,000	15,000
Operating profit	-119,760	115,500	259,100
EBITDA	-114,760	130,500	274,100
Financial income and expenses	-5,250	-30,448	-25,569
Profit before income tax	-125,010	85,052	233,531
Income tax expense	-12,501	8,505	23,353
Profit	-112,509	76,547	210,178
Operating margin	-9.58%	4.25%	8.58%
Gross margin	74.7%	75%	75.1%
Sales per employee	106,818	138,462	163,333
Value added	612,500	1,027,500	1,385,000
Value added per employee	55,682	79,038	92,333
Return on equity (per year)	-500%	48.1%	60.2%
Quick ratio	1.04	0.90	8.52
Current ratio	1.04	0.90	8.52
ISCR	-21.9	4.29	10.7
DSCR	0	1.08	1.79
Debt to equity ratio	3.33	3.04	1.02
Debt to capital ratio	76.9%	75.3%	50.5%
Receivables collection period, days	15.0	15.0	15.0

Payable period, days	15.0	15.0	15.0

Income statements (USD)

	2012	2013	2014
Sales revenue	1,175,000	1,800,000	2,450,000
Cost of sales	297,500	450,000	610,000
Other operating expenses	265,000	322,500	455,000
Labor cost			
Wages and salaries	632,400	780,000	966,000
Social security costs	94,860	117,000	144,900
Total labour cost	727,260	897,000	1,110,900
Depreciation of fixed assets	5,000	15,000	15,000
Operating profit	-119,760	115,500	259,100
Financial expenses			
Interest expense	5,250	30,448	25,569
Total financial expenses	5,250	30,448	25,569
Profit before income tax	-125,010	85,052	233,531
Income tax expense	-12,501	8,505	23,353
Net profit for financial year	-112,509	76,547	210,178

Balance sheets (USD)

	2012	2013	2014

ASSETS

Current assets

Cash	3,422	52,939	114,404
Receivables and prepayments			
Trade receivables	48,968	75,006	102,087
Prepaid and deferred taxes	12,501	3,996	0.00
Inventories			
Inventories	0	0	0
Total current assets	64,890	131,940	216,491
Fixed assets			
Tangible assets			
Machineny and equipment	50,000	550,000	550,000
Less: Accumulated depreciation	-5,000	-20,000	-35,000
Total	45,000	530,000	515,000
Total fixed assets	45,000	530,000	515,000
Total assets	109,890	661,940	731,491
LIABILITIES and OWNERS' EQUITY			
Liabilities			
Current liabilities			
Loan liabilities			
Short-term loans and notes	0	0	0
Current portion of long-term loan liabilities	50,000	127,295	0
Total	50,000	127,295	0
Debts and prepayments			

Trade creditors, goods	12,399	18,751	25,418
Trade creditors, other	0	0	0
Employee-related liabilities	0	0	0
Total	12,399	18,751	25,418
Total current liabilities	62,399	146,046	25,418
Long-term liabilities			
Long-term loan liabilities			
Loans, notes and financial lease payables	25,000	356,857	356,857
Total long-term liabilities	25,000	356,857	356,857
Total liabilities	87,399	502,902	382,275
Owners' equity			
Share capital in nominal value	135,000	195,000	195,000
Share premium	0	0	0
Retained profit/loss	0	-112,509	-55,962
Current year profit	-112,509	76,547	210,178
Total owners' equity	22,491	159,038	349,216
Total liabilities and owners' equity	109,890	661,940	731,491

Cash flow statement (USD)

	Q3-2012	Q4-2012	Q1-2013	Q2-2013
CASH FLOWS FROM OPERATING ACTIVITIES				
Inflows				
Payments from customers	293,745	293,755	423,965	449,997

Total	293,745	293,755	423,965	449,997

Outflows

Payments to vendors (goods)	74,373	74,377	106,149	112,499
Payment of salaries and wages	158,100	158,100	195,000	195,000
Social security costs	23,715	23,715	29,250	29,250
Payments to vendors (operating expenses)	58,743	58,771	80,622	80,622
Total	314,931	314,963	411,021	417,371
Net cash flow from operating activities	-21,186	-21,208	12,944	32,626
Payments to vendors (goods)		285,101	443,648	603,333
Payment of salaries and wages		632,400	780,000	966,000
Social security costs		94,860	117,000	144,900
Payments to vendors (operating expenses)		265,000	322,500	455,000
Total		1,277,361	1,663,148	2,169,233
Net cash flow from operating activities		-151,328	110,814	253,686

See other Attachments

Sample – Nonprofit Grant Proposal and Process

(Provided by UNC Chapel Hill)

What this handout is about

This handout will help you write and revise grant proposals for research funding in all academic disciplines (sciences, social sciences, humanities, and the arts). It's targeted primarily to graduate students and faculty, although it will also be helpful to undergraduate students who are seeking funding for research (e.g. for a senior thesis).

The grant writing process

Grant writing varies widely across the disciplines, and research intended for epistemological purposes (philosophy or the arts) rests on very different assumptions than research intended for practical applications (medicine or social policy research). Nonetheless, this handout attempts to provide a general introduction to grant writing across the disciplines.

Although some scholars in the humanities and arts may not have thought about their projects in terms of research design, hypotheses, research questions, or results, reviewers and funding agencies expect you to frame your project in these terms. Learning the language of grant writing can be a lucrative endeavor, so give it a try. You may also find that thinking about your project in these terms reveals new aspects of it to you.

Writing successful grant applications is a long process that begins with an idea. Although many people think of grant writing as a linear process (from idea to proposal to award), it is a circular process. Diagram 1 below provides an overview of the grant writing process and may help you plan your proposal development.

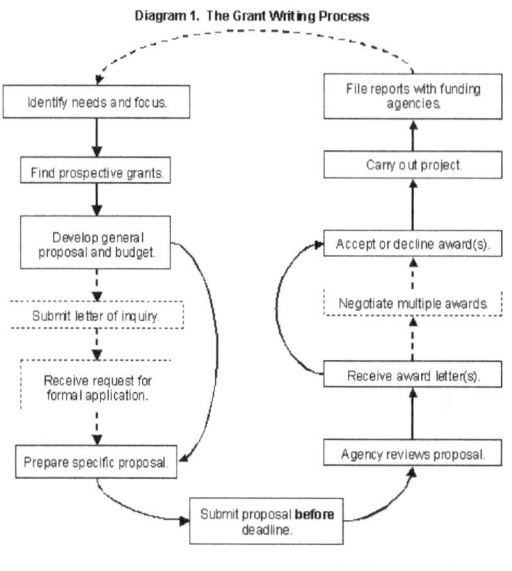

Diagram 1. The Grant Writing Process

Applicants must write grant proposals, submit them, receive notice of acceptance or rejection, and then revise their proposals. Unsuccessful grant applicants must revise and resubmit their proposals during the next funding cycle. Successful grant applications and the resulting research lead to ideas for further research and new grant proposals.

Cultivating an ongoing, positive relationship with funding agencies may lead to additional grants down the road. Thus, make sure you file progress reports and final reports in a timely and professional manner. Although some successful grant applicants may fear that funding agencies will reject future proposals because they've already received "enough" funding, the truth is that money follows money. Individuals or projects awarded grants in the past are more competitive and thus more likely to receive funding in the future.

Some general tips

Begin early.

Apply early and often.

Don't forget to include a cover letter with your application.

Answer all questions. (Pre-empt all unstated questions.)

If rejected, revise your proposal and apply again.

Give them what they want. Follow the application guidelines exactly.

>Be explicit and specific.

>Be realistic in designing the project.

>Make explicit the connections between your research questions and objectives, your objectives and methods, your methods and results, and your results and dissemination plan.

>Follow the application guidelines exactly. (We have repeated this tip because it is very, very important.)

>Before you start writing Identify your needs and focus

Answering the following questions may help you:

>Are you undertaking preliminary or pilot research in order to develop a full-blown research agenda?

>Are you seeking funding for dissertation research? Pre-dissertation research? Postdoctoral research? Archival research? Experimental research? Fieldwork?

>Are you seeking a stipend so that you can write a dissertation or book? Polish a manuscript?

>Do you want a fellowship in residence at an institution that will offer some programmatic support or other resources to enhance your project?

>Do you want funding for a large research project that will last for several years and involve multiple staff members?

Next, think about the focus of your research/project. Answering the following questions may help you narrow it down:

>What is the topic? Why is this topic important?

>What are the research questions that you're trying to answer? What relevance do your research questions have?

>What are your hypotheses?

>What are your research methods?

> Why is your research/project important? What is its significance?
>
> Do you plan on using quantitative methods? Qualitative methods? Both?
>
> Will you be undertaking experimental research? Clinical research?

Once you have identified your needs and focus, you can begin looking for prospective grants and funding agencies.

Finding prospective grants and funding agencies

Whether your proposal receives funding will rely in large part on whether your purpose and goals closely match the priorities of granting agencies. Locating possible grantors is a time consuming task, but in the long run it will yield the greatest benefits. Even if you have the most appealing research proposal in the world, if you don't send it to the right institutions, then you're unlikely to receive funding.

There are many sources of information about granting agencies and grant programs. Most universities and many schools within universities have Offices of Research, whose primary purpose is to support faculty and students in grant-seeking endeavors. These offices usually have libraries or resource centers to help people find prospective grants.

At UNC, the Research at Carolina office coordinates research support.

The Grant Source Library, located in Bynum Hall, provides grant-seeking assistance to UNC students and faculty. The Grant Source Library maintains a wide variety of resources (books, journals, and online databases) and offers workshops to help students and faculty find funding.

The UNC Medical School and School of Public Health each have their own Office of Research.

Writing your proposal

Audience

The majority of grant programs recruit academic reviewers with knowledge of the disciplines and/or program areas of the grant. Thus, when writing your grant proposals, assume that you are addressing a colleague who is knowledgeable in the general area, but who does not necessarily know the details about your research questions.

Remember that most readers are lazy and will not respond well to a poorly organized, poorly written, or confusing proposal. Be sure to give readers what they want. Follow all the guidelines for the particular grant you are applying for. This may require you to reframe your project in a different light or language. Reframing your project to fit a specific grant's requirements is a legitimate and necessary part of the process unless it will fundamentally change your project's goals or outcomes.

Final decisions about which proposals are funded often come down to whether the proposal convinces the reviewer that the research project is well planned and feasible and whether the investigators are well qualified to execute it. Throughout the proposal, be as explicit as possible. Predict the questions that the reviewer may have and answer them. Przeworski and Salomon (1995) note that reviewers read with three questions in mind:

> What are we going to learn as a result of the proposed project that we do not know now? (goals, aims, and outcomes)
>
> Why is it worth knowing? (Significance)
>
> How will we know that the conclusions are valid? (Criteria for success) (2)

Be sure to answer these questions in your proposal. Keep in mind that the reviewer may not read every word of your proposal. He/she may only read the abstract, the sections on research design and methodology, the vitae, and the budget. Make these sections as clear and straight forward as possible.

Style

The way you write your grant will tell the reviewers a lot about you (Reif-Lehrer 82). From reading your proposal, the reviewers will form an idea of who you are as a scholar, a researcher, and a person. They will decide whether you are creative, logical, analytical, up-to-date in the relevant literature of the field, and, most importantly, capable of executing the proposed project. Allow your discipline and its conventions to determine the general style of your writing, but allow your own voice and personality to come through. Be sure to clarify your project's theoretical orientation.

Develop a general proposal and budget

Because most proposal writers seek funding from several different agencies or granting programs, it is a good idea to begin by developing a general grant proposal and budget. This general proposal is sometimes called a "white paper." Your general proposal should explain your project to a general academic audience. Before you submit proposals to different grant programs, you will tailor a specific proposal to their guidelines and priorities.

Organizing your proposal

Although each funding agency will have its own (usually very specific) requirements, there are several elements of a proposal that are fairly standard, and they often come in the following order:

Title page

Abstract

Introduction (statement of the problem, purpose of research or goals, and significance of research)

Literature review

Project narrative (methods, procedures, objectives, outcomes or deliverables, evaluation, and dissemination)

Personnel

Budget and budget justification

Format the proposal so that it is easy to read. Use headings to break the proposal up into sections. If it is long, include a table of contents with page numbers.

Title page

The title page usually includes a brief yet explicit title for the research project, the names of the principal investigator(s), the institutional affiliation of the applicants (the department and university), name and address of the granting agency, project dates, amount of funding requested, and signatures of university personnel authorizing the proposal (when necessary). Most funding agencies have specific requirements for the title page; make sure to follow them.

Abstract

The abstract provides readers with their first impression of your project. To remind themselves of your proposal, readers may glance at your abstract when making their final recommendations, so it may also serve as their last impression of your project. The abstract should explain the key elements of your research project in the future tense. Most abstracts state: (1) the general purpose, (2) specific goals, (3) research design, (4) methods, and (5) significance (contribution and rationale). Be as explicit as possible in your abstract. Use statements such as, "The objective of this study is to …"

Introduction

The introduction should cover the key elements of your proposal, including a statement of the problem, the purpose of research, research goals or objectives, and significance of the research. The statement of problem should provide a background and rationale for the project and establish the need and relevance of the research. How is your project different from previous research on the same topic? Will you be using new methodologies or covering new theoretical territory? The research goals or objectives should identify the anticipated outcomes of the research and should match up to the needs identified in the statement of problem. List only the principle goal(s) or objective(s) of your research and save sub-objectives for the project narrative.

Literature review

Many proposals require a literature review. Reviewers want to know whether you've done the necessary preliminary research to undertake your project. Literature reviews should be selective and critical, not exhaustive. Reviewers want to see your evaluation of pertinent works. For more information, see our handout on literature reviews.

Project narrative

The project narrative provides the meat of your proposal and may require several subsections. The project narrative should supply all the details of the project, including a detailed statement of problem, research objectives or goals, hypotheses, methods, procedures, outcomes or deliverables, and evaluation and dissemination of the research.

For the project narrative, pre-empt and/or answer all of the reviewers' questions. Don't leave them wondering about anything. For example, if you propose to conduct unstructured interviews with open-ended questions, be sure you've explained why this methodology is best suited to the specific research questions in your proposal. Or, if you're using item response theory rather than classical test theory to verify the validity of your survey instrument, explain the advantages of this innovative methodology. Or, if you need to travel to Valdez, Alaska to access historical archives at the Valdez Museum, make it clear what documents you hope to find and why they are relevant to your historical novel on the '98ers in the Alaskan Gold Rush.

Clearly and explicitly state the connections between your research objectives, research questions, hypotheses, methodologies, and outcomes. As the requirements for a strong project narrative vary widely by discipline, consult a discipline-specific guide to grant writing for some additional advice.

Personnel

Explain staffing requirements in detail and make sure that staffing makes sense. Be very explicit about the skill sets of the personnel already in place (you will probably include their Curriculum Vitae as part of the proposal). Explain the necessary skill sets and functions of personnel you will recruit. To minimize expenses, phase out personnel who are not relevant to later phases of a project.

Budget

The budget spells out project costs and usually consists of a spreadsheet or table with the budget detailed as line items and a budget narrative (also known as a budget justification) that explains the various expenses. Even when proposal guidelines do not specifically mention a narrative, be sure to include a one or two page explanation of the budget. To see a sample budget, turn to Example #1 at the end of this handout.

Consider including an exhaustive budget for your project, even if it exceeds the normal grant size of a particular funding organization. Simply make it clear that you are seeking additional funding from other sources. This technique will make it easier for you to combine awards down the road should you have the good fortune of receiving multiple grants.

Make sure that all budget items meet the funding agency's requirements. For example, all U.S. government agencies have strict requirements for airline travel. Be sure the cost of the airline travel in your budget meets their requirements. If a line item falls outside an agency's requirements (e.g. some organizations will not cover equipment purchases or other capital expenses), explain in the budget justification that other grant sources will pay for the item.

Many universities require that indirect costs (overhead) be added to grants that they administer. Check with the appropriate offices to find out what the standard (or required) rates are for overhead. Pass a draft budget by the university officer in charge of grant administration for assistance with indirect costs and costs not directly associated with research (e.g. facilities use charges).

Timeframe

Explain the timeframe for the research project in some detail. When will you begin and complete each step? It may be helpful to reviewers if you present a visual version of your timeline. For less complicated research, a table summarizing the timeline for the project will help reviewers understand and evaluate the planning and feasibility. See Example #2 at the end of this handout.

For multi-year research proposals with numerous procedures and a large staff, a time line diagram can help clarify the feasibility and planning of the study. See Example #3 at the end of this handout.

Revising your proposal

Strong grant proposals take a long time to develop. Start the process early and leave time to get feedback from several readers on different drafts. Seek out a variety of readers, both specialists in your research area and non-specialist colleagues. You may also want to request assistance from knowledgeable readers on specific areas of your proposal. For example, you may want to schedule a meeting with a statistician to help revise your methodology section. Don't hesitate to seek out specialized assistance from the relevant research offices on your campus. At UNC, the Odum Institute provides a variety of services to graduate students and faculty in the social sciences.

In your revision and editing, ask your readers to give careful consideration to whether you've made explicit the connections between your research objectives and methodology. Here are some example questions:

> Have you presented a compelling case?

> Have you made your hypotheses explicit?

> Does your project seem feasible? Is it overly ambitious? Does it have other weaknesses?

> Have you stated the means that grantors can use to evaluate the success of your project after you've executed it?

If a granting agency lists particular criteria used for rating and evaluating proposals, be sure to share these with your own reviewers.

Example #1. Sample Budget

Item

Quantity

	Cost	Subtotal	Total
Jet Travel			
RDU-Kigali (roundtrip) 1		$6,100	$6,100
Maintenance Allowance			
Rwanda 12 months	$1,899	$22,788	$22,788
Project Allowance			
Research Assistant/Translator 12 months	$400	$4800	
Transportation within country			
–Phase 1 4 months	$300	$1,200	
–Phase 2 8 months	$1,500	$12,000	
Email 12 months	$60	$720	
Audio cassette tapes 200	$2	$400	
Photographic and slide film 20	$5	$100	
Laptop Computer 1		$2,895	
NUD*IST 4.0 Software		$373	
Etc.			
Total Project Allowance		$35,238	
Administrative Fee		$100	
Total	$65,690		
Sought from other sources		($15,000)	
Total Grant Request		$50,690	

Jet travel $6,100

This estimate is based on the commercial high season rate for jet economy travel on Sabena Belgian Airlines. No U.S. carriers fly to Kigali, Rwanda. Sabena has student fare tickets available which will be significantly less expensive (approximately $2,000).

Maintenance allowance $22,788

Based on the Fulbright-Hays Maintenance Allowances published in the grant application guide.

Research assistant/translator $4,800

The research assistant/translator will be a native (and primary) speaker of Kinya-rwanda with at least a four-year university degree. He/she will accompany the primary investigator during life history interviews to provide assistance in comprehension. In addition, he/she will provide commentary, explanations, and observations to facilitate the primary investigator's participant observation. During the first phase of the project in Kigali, the research assistant will work forty hours a week and occasional overtime as needed. During phases two and three in rural Rwanda, the assistant will stay with the investigator overnight in the field when necessary. The salary of $400 per month is based on the average pay rate for individuals with similar qualifications working for international NGO's in Rwanda.

Transportation within country, phase one $1,200

The primary investigator and research assistant will need regular transportation within Kigali by bus and taxi. The average taxi fare in Kigali is $6-8 and bus fare is $.15. This figure is based on an average of $10 per day in transportation costs during the first project phase.

Transportation within country, phases two and three $12,000

Project personnel will also require regular transportation between rural field sites. If it is not possible to remain overnight, daily trips will be necessary. The average rental rate for a 4×4 vehicle in Rwanda is $130 per day. This estimate is based on an average of $50 per day in transportation costs for the second and third project phases. These costs could be reduced if an arrangement could be made with either a government ministry or international aid agency for transportation assistance.

Email $720

The rate for email service from RwandaTel (the only service provider in Rwanda) is $60 per month. Email access is vital for receiving news reports on Rwanda and the region as well as for staying in contact with dissertation committee members and advisors in the United States.

Audiocassette tapes $400

Audiocassette tapes will be necessary for recording life history interviews, musical performances, community events, story telling, and other pertinent data.

Photographic & slide film $100

Photographic and slide film will be necessary to document visual data such as landscape, environment, marriages, funerals, community events, etc.

Laptop computer $2,895

A laptop computer will be necessary for recording observations, thoughts, and analysis during research project. Price listed is a special offer to UNC students through the Carolina Computing Initiative.

NUD*IST 4.0 software $373.00

NUD*IST, "Nonnumerical, Unstructured Data, Indexing, Searching, and Theorizing," is necessary for cataloging, indexing, and managing field notes both during and following the field research phase. The program will assist in cataloging themes that emerge during the life history interviews.

Administrative fee $100

Fee set by Fulbright-Hays for the sponsoring institution.

Example #2: Project Timeline in Table Format

Exploratory Research	Completed
Proposal Development	Completed
Ph.D. qualifying exams	Completed
Research Proposal Defense	Completed
Fieldwork in Rwanda	Oct. 1999-Dec. 2000

Data Analysis and Transcription   Jan. 2001-March 2001

Writing of Draft Chapters   March 2001 – Sept. 2001

Revision   Oct. 2001-Feb. 2002

Dissertation Defense   April 2002

Final Approval and Completion   May 2002

Example #3: Project Timeline in Chart Format

Activity	GY1				GY2			
	Q1	Q2	Q3	Q4	Q5	Q6	Q7	Q8
• Develop items for survey	■							
• Review and revise items with experts' panel.		■	■					
• Pre-test items with representative sample of target population.		■						
• Program software to administer survey.			■					
• Prepare survey sites for study.			■					
• Recruit and train Study Reps.			■					
• Recruit 1,000 subjects and administer survey at 5 sites.				■	■	■		
• Statistical analysis of data.							■	■
• Preparation and submission of manuscripts to peer-reviewed journals.								■

Some closing advice

   Some of us may feel ashamed or embarrassed about asking for money or promoting ourselves. Often, these feelings have more to do with our own insecurities than with problems in the tone or style of our writing. If you're having trouble because of these types of hang-ups, the most important thing to keep in mind is that it never hurts to ask. If you never ask for the money, they'll never give you the money. Besides, the worst thing they can do is say no.

Other books in this series of The Housewives Guide to becoming Wealthy are:

The Housewives Guide to becoming Wealthy by working at Home

Available in paperback and on ebook format on Amazon, Barnes and Noble, Lulu, and other fine bookstores worldwide

- **ISBN-10:** 1548845485
- **ISBN-13:** 978-1548845483

Other book subjects to be published in 2018 in this Series are:

Contracts, Letters and Forms

For Profit Corporations

Non-Profit Corporations

Establishing Business Credit

Goals Planner

Our Future: Trade Jobs

www.ingramcontent.com/pod-product-compliance
Lightning Source LLC
Chambersburg PA
CBHW062223220526
45471CB00009B/3323